DAILY

DEVOTIONAL

FOR MEN

Published by Midsummer Bloom Books

First Edition: August 2025
Printed in the United States of America.

CONTENTS

INTRODUCTION

Welcome, brother. This book in your hands isn't just another devotional—it's a daily conversation between you, God's Word, and the reality of being a man in today's world. Whether you're grabbing coffee before dawn, taking a lunch break, or winding down after putting the kids to bed, these pages are designed to meet you right where you are. Life throws curveballs. Some days you're crushing it at work, other days you're wondering if you're enough—as a husband, father, friend, or follower of Christ. This devotional doesn't pretend those struggles don't exist. Instead, it dives straight into them with the timeless wisdom of Scripture and the transforming power of God's grace. Each day offers a verse, a reflection that connects God's truth to your everyday life, and a question to carry with you. No religious jargon, no impossible standards—just real talk about real faith for real men. Start anywhere. Miss a day? No guilt trips here. Just pick up where you left off. God's mercies are new every morning, and His Word remains powerful whether you're on Day 1 or Day 365. Let's walk this journey together, one day at a time.

January: Foundations of Faith

Day 1

"In the beginning God created the heaven and the earth." — *Genesis 1:1 (KJV)*

Every great story starts somewhere, and yours is no exception. Before your first breath, before your parents met, before the foundations of the world, God was already writing your story. That project that's keeping you up at night? That relationship you're trying to figure out? The God who spoke galaxies into existence knows every detail. Starting fresh feels different when you remember who's holding the pen. Today isn't just another January 1st—it's a page in the story God is telling through your life. The same power that brought order from chaos in creation can bring order to whatever feels chaotic in your world right now.

Reflection Question: What area of your life needs God's creative power to bring order from chaos?

DAY 2

"And God said, Let there be light: and there was light." — Genesis 1:3 (KJV)

God's first recorded words brought light into darkness. Not a suggestion, not a wish—a command that darkness had no choice but to obey. That same voice speaks into your darkness today. The depression that clouds your mornings, the confusion about your next career move, the loneliness despite being surrounded by people—none of it can stand against His light. Notice God didn't eliminate darkness; He created light to overcome it. Your struggles won't magically disappear, but His light changes how you navigate through them. Like switching on headlights on a dark highway, suddenly you can see the next few feet ahead, and that's enough.

Reflection Question: Where do you need God's light to break through darkness in your life today?

DAY 3

"So God created man in his own image, in the image of God created he him." — Genesis 1:27 (KJV)

You bear God's image. Let that sink in. Not just on your good days when you're patient with your kids or generous with your time. Even on days when you lose your temper in traffic or fall short of your own expectations, you carry the fingerprint of the Almighty. This truth changes everything about how you see yourself and others. That difficult coworker? Image bearer. The man in the mirror you're sometimes hard on? Image bearer. You were crafted with intention, not mass-produced. Your creativity, your desire for purpose, your capacity to love—all reflections of your Maker.

Reflection Question: How would your day change if you truly believed you bear God's image?

DAY 4

"And the Lord God said, It is not good that the man should be alone." — *Genesis 2:18 (KJV)*

God created you for connection. In a world that celebrates the lone wolf and the self-made man, Scripture says something radical: you need others. Not just a wife or girlfriend, but genuine brotherhood—men who know your struggles and still show up. Isolation is where the enemy does his best work. When you're alone with your thoughts, fears multiply and problems seem insurmountable. But in community, burdens get lighter and victories taste sweeter. That text you've been meaning to send to check on a friend? Send it. That men's group you've been avoiding? Give it a shot.

Reflection Question: Who in your life needs to hear from you today, and who do you need to reach out to for support?

DAY 5

"And on the seventh day God ended his work which he had made; and he rested." — *Genesis 2:2 (KJV)*

If God rested, what makes you think you don't need to? The Creator of the universe, who never grows tired, demonstrated rest. Not because He was exhausted, but because rest is part of the rhythm of life He designed. Yet here you are, wearing busyness like a badge of honor. Rest isn't laziness; it's trust. It's saying, "God, You can handle what I'm setting down." It's believing the world won't fall apart if you take a break. Your worth isn't measured by your productivity. Sometimes the most spiritual thing you can do is take a nap, play catch with your kids, or simply sit still.

Reflection Question: What would it look like to build intentional rest into your life this week?

DAY 6

"And Enoch walked with God: and he was not; for God took him." —
Genesis 5:24 (KJV)

Enoch's entire biography boils down to this: he walked with
God. Not ran or crawled—walked. A steady, daily pace of
fellowship, with no record of parting seas or slaying giants,
just faithfully showing up. Walking means going somewhere
together, matching pace, and having conversations along the
way. God isn't seeking spiritual sprinters who burn out but
walking partners for the long haul. Your faith doesn't need to
be flashy to be real. Sometimes the most powerful testimony
is simply showing up, day after day.

*Reflection Question: What would "walking with God" look like
in your daily routine?*

DAY 7

"By faith Abel offered unto God a more excellent sacrifice than Cain." —
Hebrews 11:4 (KJV)

Abel's offering wasn't better because of superior livestock
or presentation—it came from faith. Cain went through the
motions; Abel brought his heart. The difference between religion and relationship is in how we give—our time, talents,
and resources. God isn't impressed by perfect attendance or
big donations if your heart's not in it. He'd rather have honest
struggles than polished pretense. That dry prayer time or
routine worship? Bring faith, even mustard-seed-sized, and
watch how it transforms the ordinary into something deeply
relational.

*Reflection Question: Where have you been going through the
motions, and how can you bring genuine faith to that area?*

DAY 8

"Thus did Noah; according to all that God commanded him, so did he." —
Genesis 6:22 (KJV)

Noah built a boat in the desert. No weather forecast, no You-Tube tutorial, just God's word and his willingness to look foolish. Every hammer strike was an act of faith while neighbors probably called him crazy. But Noah understood something: obedience doesn't require understanding, it requires trust. God might be asking you to build something that doesn't make sense yet—a career change, a reconciliation, a new habit. The blueprint might seem unclear, and people might not understand. But partial obedience is disobedience. Noah didn't build half an ark. Whatever God's asking of you, do all of it.

Reflection Question: What has God asked you to do that you've been putting off because it doesn't make complete sense?

DAY 9

"I do set my bow in the cloud, and it shall be for a token of a covenant between me and the earth." — *Genesis 9:13 (KJV)*

After the storm comes the promise. God didn't just tell Noah He'd never flood the earth again; He painted it across the sky. Every rainbow is God's signature on His promise, a reminder that He keeps His word even when we don't deserve it. You've weathered storms—job losses, relationship failures, health scares. Maybe you're in one right now. Look for the rainbow, not as wishful thinking but as evidence of God's faithfulness. His promises aren't canceled by your circumstances. The same God who brought Noah through the flood is navigating you through yours.

Reflection Question: What promises of God do you need to remember and hold onto today?

DAY 10

"Now the Lord had said unto Abram, Get thee out of thy country...unto a land that I will shew thee." — Genesis 12:1 (KJV)

God called Abraham to leave everything familiar for a destination marked "to be revealed." No GPS coordinates, no five-year plan, just "go, and I'll show you." Following God often means moving forward before you can see the whole path. That comfort zone you're clinging to might be the very thing keeping you from God's promises. Abraham could have stayed in Ur, safe and settled. Instead, he chose uncertainty with God over security without Him. Your next chapter might require leaving what's familiar—a job, a mindset, a relationship—trusting that God's "I will show you" is enough.

Reflection Question: What comfortable place might God be calling you to leave in order to follow Him more fully?

DAY 11

"And he believed in the Lord; and he counted it to him for righteousness." — Genesis 15:6 (KJV)

Abraham didn't earn God's approval through perfect behavior. He simply believed God's promise, and that faith was credited as righteousness. In a world that measures worth by achievement, God says your faith in Him is what counts. Stop trying to earn what's already been given. Your mistakes don't disqualify you, and your successes don't qualify you. God's not keeping score the way you think He is. Abraham had doubts, made mistakes, and still became the father of faith. Your belief, even when shaky, is precious to God.

Reflection Question: Where have you been trying to earn God's approval instead of simply believing His promises?

DAY 12

"And Sarah said, God hath made me to laugh, so that all that hear will laugh with me." — Genesis 21:6 (KJV)

Sarah's laughter transformed from skepticism to joy. The same promise that once seemed impossible became her greatest testimony. God specializes in turning our doubts into dancing, our questions into testimonies. That thing you've given up on—the marriage restoration, the prodigal child's return, the breakthrough you've stopped expecting—God hasn't forgotten. He's not bound by biological clocks or human limitations. Sarah held her promise at 90. Your timeline isn't God's timeline, but His timing is always perfect.

Reflection Question: What impossible situation do you need to trust God with, even if it seems too late?

DAY 13

"And he said, Take now thy son, thine only son Isaac, whom thou lovest...and offer him." — Genesis 22:2 (KJV)

God asked Abraham to sacrifice what he loved most. Not because God wanted Isaac dead, but because He wanted Abraham's heart fully alive to Him. Sometimes God asks us to lay down our Isaacs—our dreams, our plans, our most precious possessions—not to take them away, but to ensure they don't take His place. What are you gripping so tightly that your knuckles are white? Your career? Your reputation? Your kids' success? Open your hands. Abraham discovered that what we're willing to sacrifice, God is able to resurrect and bless beyond imagination.

Reflection Question: What "Isaac" in your life needs to be surrendered to God's altar?

DAY 14

"And Jacob was left alone; and there wrestled a man with him until the breaking of the day." — Genesis 32:24 (KJV)

Jacob wrestled with God all night and walked away with a limp and a blessing. Sometimes faith isn't peaceful; it's a wrestling match. Those nights when you can't sleep, arguing with God about His plan, questioning His methods—that's not lack of faith. That's engagement. God can handle your wrestling. He'd rather have your honest struggle than your distant politeness. Jacob wouldn't let go until he got his blessing. That tenacious faith, even when it feels like fighting, moves God's heart. Your spiritual limp might be the evidence of an encounter that changed everything.

Reflection Question: What are you wrestling with God about, and how might that struggle actually be deepening your faith?

DAY 15

"But the Lord was with Joseph, and shewed him mercy, and gave him favour in the sight of the keeper of the prison." — Genesis 39:21 (KJV)

Joseph found favor in prison. Not in the palace he probably dreamed about, but in the last place anyone would choose. Sometimes God's presence is most evident in life's prisons—those circumstances you didn't choose and can't escape. Your prison might be a dead-end job, a difficult marriage, or a health condition. Joseph teaches us that you can bloom where you're planted, even in concrete. God's favor isn't limited by your circumstances. He's working even in the waiting room, preparing you for purposes you can't see yet.

Reflection Question: How can you find and show God's favor in your current "prison" situation?

DAY 16

"But as for you, ye thought evil against me; but God meant it unto good."
— Genesis 50:20 (KJV)

Joseph looked at brothers who sold him into slavery and saw God's providence instead of seeking revenge. That's supernatural perspective. The betrayals you've experienced, the unfair treatment, the wounds that still ache—God's not surprised by any of it. Forgiveness isn't saying what happened was okay; it's saying God is bigger than what happened. Joseph could see God's hand in his brothers' betrayal because he chose to look for it. Your worst chapters might be preparing you for your best ministry. What others meant for evil, God is already transforming for good.

Reflection Question: Who do you need to forgive, trusting that God can redeem even their worst actions?

DAY 17

"And Moses said unto the Lord, O my Lord, I am not eloquent...I am slow of speech." — Exodus 4:10 (KJV)

Moses had every excuse ready. Not qualified, not eloquent, not the right guy. Sound familiar? God doesn't call the qualified; He qualifies the called. Your inadequacies aren't news to God— He factored them in when He chose you. Stop disqualifying yourself from what God has qualified you for. Moses thought his stuttering would stop God's plan. Instead, God gave him Aaron and used both their weaknesses for His glory. Your limitations might be the very thing that makes room for God's power to be obvious.

Reflection Question: What excuse have you been using to avoid what God is calling you to do?

DAY 18

"Fear ye not, stand still, and see the salvation of the Lord." — Exodus 14:13 (KJV)

With the Red Sea ahead and Pharaoh's army behind, God said: stand still. Not run, fight, or swim—stand still. Sometimes the most active faith looks like waiting. When you're trapped between impossible and more impossible, that's when God does His best work. Your instinct is to do something, anything. But God's instruction might be to be still and watch Him work. That job situation that has no solution? That financial pressure with no relief in sight? Stand still doesn't mean give up. It means give God room to show up.

Reflection Question: Where do you need to stop striving and start trusting God to part the waters?

DAY 19

"And when the dew that lay was gone up, behold, upon the face of the wilderness there lay a small round thing." — Exodus 16:14 (KJV)

Manna came daily, not weekly or monthly. God wanted Israel to trust Him one day at a time. You want the whole month's provision in advance, but God provides daily bread because He wants daily relationship. That's why your prayers for next year's provision might go unanswered while today's needs are met. God's not being stingy; He's being relational. He wants you to wake up tomorrow needing Him again. Your daily dependence isn't weakness—it's exactly how He designed it to work.

Reflection Question: How can you practice trusting God for today's provision without worrying about tomorrow's?

DAY 20

"And God spake all these words, saying, I am the Lord thy God." — Exodus 20:1-2 (KJV)

Before giving commandments, God established relationship: "I am the Lord your God." Rules without relationship lead to rebellion, but relationship makes rules feel like protection. God's commands aren't meant to restrict freedom but to protect purpose, like guardrails on a mountain road keeping you from disaster. Every boundary comes from love, not control. When you see His commands as coming from a loving Father, obedience becomes a response to love, not religious duty. It's about trust, not just rules.

Reflection Question: Which of God's commands have you been viewing as restriction rather than protection?

DAY 21

"And when the people saw that Moses delayed to come down out of the mount, they gathered themselves...and said...make us gods." — Exodus 32:1 (KJV)

Forty days. That's how long it took for Israel to create a replacement god. When God seems delayed, the temptation is to create our own solutions. That golden calf might look like trying to control outcomes, finding comfort in addiction, or making success your god. Waiting on God tests what you really worship. When prayers seem unanswered and heaven feels silent, what substitutes do you craft? Israel's problem wasn't just idolatry; it was impatience. They wanted a god they could see and control. Sometimes faith means worshiping through the waiting.

Reflection Question: What "golden calves" do you tend to create when God seems silent or slow?

DAY 22

"And Moses besought the Lord his God, and said, Lord, why doth thy wrath wax hot against thy people?" — Exodus 32:11 (KJV)

Moses stood between God's wrath and Israel's rebellion, pleading for people who deserved judgment. That's the power of intercession—standing in the gap for others. Your prayers might be the only thing standing between someone and their consequences. Who needs you to stand in the gap today? Your wayward child, struggling friend, difficult boss? Moses reminds us that one person's prayers can change the trajectory of many lives. Don't underestimate your role as an intercessor. Someone's breakthrough might be waiting on your prayer.

Reflection Question: Who has God placed on your heart to intercede for, even if they don't deserve it?

DAY 23

"And he said, My presence shall go with thee, and I will give thee rest." — Exodus 33:14 (KJV)

Moses wouldn't take a step without God's presence. Smart man. Success without God's presence is failure, but failure with His presence is just a detour to victory. God's presence changes everything about the journey. You can have all the resources, connections, and opportunities, but without His presence, you're walking alone. Moses chose God's presence over comfort, safety, and predictability. That promotion that requires compromising your faith? That relationship that pulls you from God? No opportunity is worth losing His presence.

Reflection Question: What decision are you facing where you need to prioritize God's presence over apparent advantages?

DAY 24

"And it came to pass...that Moses wist not that the skin of his face shone while he talked with him." — Exodus 34:29 (KJV)

Moses didn't know his face was glowing. Time with God changes you in ways you don't even realize. Others notice something different—a peace during chaos, joy despite circumstances, wisdom beyond experience. You can't fake the glow that comes from God's presence. You might not feel particularly spiritual, but time with God leaves marks others can see. That coworker asking what's different about you? That's the residue of this morning's prayer time. Don't underestimate how your time with God impacts those around you, even when you feel unchanged.

Reflection Question: How might your time with God be impacting others in ways you haven't noticed?

DAY 25

"I call heaven and earth to record this day against you, that I have set before you life and death...therefore choose life." — Deuteronomy 30:19 (KJV)

God lays out the options and then tells you which one to pick. He's not neutral about your choices. Every day you're choosing between life and death in small decisions—what you watch, how you speak, where you invest your time. Choosing life isn't always the easy choice. Sometimes death looks like comfort, and life looks like hard work. That conversation you're avoiding, that habit you need to break, that forgiveness you need to extend—these are choices between life and death. God's rooting for you to choose life.

Reflection Question: What area of your life needs you to actively choose life instead of settling for slow death?

DAY 26

"Be strong and of a good courage; fear not, nor be afraid of them: for the Lord thy God, he it is that doth go with thee." — Deuteronomy 31:6 (KJV)

God commands courage, not because the situation isn't scary, but because He's with you. Courage isn't the absence of fear; it's moving forward despite fear because you know Who's walking beside you. That conversation you're dreading, that risk you need to take, that stand you need to make—God's not asking you to feel brave. He's asking you to be obedient while He handles the rest. His presence is your courage. You don't need to conjure up strength; you need to remember Whose you are.

Reflection Question: Where is God calling you to be courageous, trusting in His presence rather than your own strength?

DAY 27

"Then sang Moses and the children of Israel this song unto the Lord." — Exodus 15:1 (KJV)

After crossing the Red Sea, before facing the wilderness, Israel stopped to sing. Worship is how we transition from one miracle to the next challenge. Don't be so quick to rush from victory to the next battle without pausing to praise. Your song of praise becomes tomorrow's reminder of God's faithfulness. When Israel faced new challenges, they could remember: we're the people who sang on the other side of the impossible. What has God brought you through that deserves a song today?

Reflection Question: What recent victory needs to be celebrated with praise before you face the next challenge?

DAY 28

"But the Lord said unto Samuel...for the Lord seeth not as man seeth; for man looketh on the outward appearance, but the Lord looketh on the heart."
— 1 Samuel 16:7 (KJV)

God's evaluation system is completely different from the world's. While everyone else is impressed by height, wealth, or achievements, God's checking your heart. David wasn't the obvious choice, but he had the right heart. Stop trying to polish your exterior while your interior needs work. That promotion you didn't get might be because God's more concerned with your character than your career. He's preparing your heart for purposes that require integrity, not just ability. Internal development determines external impact.

Reflection Question: What heart issue is God working on that's more important than external success?

DAY 29

"And David said to the Philistine, Thou comest to me with a sword...but I come to thee in the name of the Lord of hosts." — 1 Samuel 17:45 (KJV)

David saw the same giant everyone else saw, but he had different perspective. While others compared Goliath's size to themselves, David compared him to God. Your giants look different when you stop measuring them against your strength and start measuring them against God's. That overwhelming debt, that impossible diagnosis, that relationship that seems beyond repair—it's not about your sword or shield. It's about whose name you're fighting in. David's victory started long before he picked up the stone. It started when he decided God was bigger.

Reflection Question: What giant do you need to face in God's name rather than your own strength?

DAY 30

"And Jonathan said to David, Go in peace, forasmuch as we have sworn both of us in the name of the Lord." — *1 Samuel 20:42 (KJV)*

Jonathan chose loyalty to David over loyalty to position. Real friendship sometimes costs you something. In a world of networking and strategic relationships, Jonathan models friendship that puts another's success above your own. Every man needs a Jonathan—someone who celebrates your victories without jealousy and stands with you when it costs them. More importantly, someone needs you to be their Jonathan. True brotherhood isn't built on convenience but on covenant. Who are you willing to stand with even when it's costly?

Reflection Question: Who in your life needs you to be a Jonathan, choosing their good over your gain?

DAY 31

"And when he had removed him, he raised up unto them David to be their king...I have found David...a man after mine own heart." — *Acts 13:22 (KJV)*

David wasn't perfect—far from it. But he was described as a man after God's heart. It wasn't his performance but his pursuit that defined him. Every time he fell, he fell forward, toward God rather than away from Him. Being after God's heart doesn't mean never failing; it means always returning. Your mistakes don't disqualify you if they drive you back to God. David's psalms weren't written from a place of perfection but from the tension of being human while hungering for the divine. That's where you are too.

Reflection Question: How can your failures become pathways back to pursuing God's heart?

FEBRUARY: LOVE AND RELATIONSHIPS

DAY 32

"And now abideth faith, hope, charity, these three; but the greatest of these is charity." — 1 Corinthians 13:13 (KJV)

Love outlasts everything. Your accomplishments will fade, your strength will diminish, but love remains. Paul says love trumps even faith and hope. In a world that values power and success, God says love is the ultimate currency. That argument with your spouse where being right feels more important than being loving? That grudge you're nursing because forgiveness feels like weakness? Love isn't soft—it's the strongest force in the universe. It's what holds everything together when everything else falls apart.

Reflection Question: Where have you been choosing being right over being loving?

DAY 33

"For God so loved the world, that he gave his only begotten Son." — John 3:16 (KJV)

God's love isn't theoretical—it's sacrificial. He didn't send a representative or a message; He sent His Son. Love acts. It doesn't just feel; it does. God's love has skin on it, scars to prove it, and an empty tomb to validate it. How does your love show up? It's easy to say "I love you" but harder to sacrifice for it. Your family doesn't just need to hear your love; they need to see it in your choices, your priorities, your presence. Love that doesn't cost you something isn't love—it's just sentiment.

Reflection Question: How can you move your love from words to costly action today?

DAY 34

"Husbands, love your wives, even as Christ also loved the church, and gave himself for it." — Ephesians 5:25 (KJV)

The bar is set impossibly high—love like Christ loved. Not when she deserves it, not when you feel like it, but consistently, sacrificially, purposefully. Christ loved the church when it was unlovable. That's your calling as a husband. This isn't about being a doormat; it's about being a servant leader. Christ's love was strong enough to rebuke and tender enough to forgive. Your wife needs both your strength and your gentleness, your protection and your vulnerability. Love her not as you want to be loved, but as she needs to be loved.

Reflection Question: What does sacrificial love look like specifically for your wife today?

DAY 35

"Train up a child in the way he should go: and when he is old, he will not depart from it." — Proverbs 22:6 (KJV)

Training implies consistency, repetition, and patience. You're not just teaching lessons; you're shaping souls. Every interaction is depositing something into your child's spiritual bank account that they'll draw from for decades. Your kids are watching how you handle failure, how you treat their mother, how you prioritize God. They'll remember your presence more than your presents. That baseball practice you're tempted to skip, that bedtime prayer you're too tired for—these moments matter more than you know.

Reflection Question: What are your children learning about God from watching your life?

DAY 36

"Therefore shall a man leave his father and his mother, and shall cleave unto his wife: and they shall be one flesh." — Genesis 2:24 (KJV)

Leaving doesn't mean abandoning; it means reprioritizing. Your wife becomes your primary human relationship. That's hard when your parents have opinions, when your buddies want the old you back, when work demands everything. Cleaving means sticking even when things get sticky. It's choosing your marriage over your comfort, your unity over your independence. Every time you choose her over easier options, you're building something that can weather any storm.

Reflection Question: What do you need to "leave" to better "cleave" to your spouse?

DAY 37

"Iron sharpeneth iron; so a man sharpeneth the countenance of his friend."
— Proverbs 27:17 (KJV)

Sharpening involves friction. Real friendship isn't always comfortable—it's constructive. You need men in your life who love you enough to tell you the truth, even when it stings. Comfort might feel better, but challenge makes you better. Who's sharpening you? If all your friendships are easy, you're probably getting dull. That accountability partner you've been avoiding, that mentor whose standards make you uncomfortable—you need them. And someone needs your sharpening influence too.

Reflection Question: Which relationship in your life needs to move from comfortable to constructive?

DAY 38

"But I say unto you, Love your enemies, bless them that curse you, do good to them that hate you." — Matthew 5:44 (KJV)

This might be the most unnatural command in Scripture. Love those who hurt you? Bless those who curse you? Everything in you wants justice, but Jesus calls for something higher—grace. That coworker undermining you, that ex-spouse making life difficult, that family member who betrayed you—Jesus says love them. Not tolerate, not ignore—love. This isn't weakness; it's warfare. You're fighting hate with love, darkness with light. It's the most powerful resistance possible.

Reflection Question: Who does God want you to love despite how they've treated you?

DAY 39

"Jesus saith unto him, I say not unto thee, Until seven times: but, Until seventy times seven." — Matthew 18:22 (KJV)

Peter thought seven times was generous. Jesus essentially said stop counting. Forgiveness isn't a limited resource; it's a lifestyle. That person who keeps hurting you, who keeps disappointing—Jesus says forgive again. This isn't about being a punching bag. It's about being free. Unforgiveness chains you to the person who hurt you. Every time you forgive, you're cutting a chain. They might not deserve it, but you deserve the freedom it brings.

Reflection Question: Who do you need to forgive for the 491st time?

DAY 40

"Bear ye one another's burdens, and so fulfil the law of Christ." — Galatians 6:2 (KJV)

Men are taught to carry their own weight, never be a burden. But God says something radical—share the load. Your struggles aren't meant to be carried alone. Pride says handle it yourself; wisdom says let others help. Bearing burdens goes both ways. While you're trying to be Superman, someone around you is drowning under a weight you could help carry. That friend going through divorce, that colleague struggling with addiction—your shoulders were built for more than just your own load.

Reflection Question: Whose burden can you help carry, and what burden do you need to share?

DAY 41

"But speaking the truth in love, that we may grow up into him in all things." — Ephesians 4:15 (KJV)

Truth without love is brutality. Love without truth is enabling. God calls for both—truth wrapped in love. That difficult conversation you're avoiding needs both honesty and compassion. Your wife needs to hear truth about how her words affect you, delivered with love. Your kids need correction that builds rather than breaks. Your friend needs someone brave enough to say what everyone else is thinking, but with grace that makes it receivable.

Reflection Question: Where do you need to balance more truth or more love in your communication?

DAY 42

"Wherefore, my beloved brethren, let every man be swift to hear, slow to speak, slow to wrath." — James 1:19 (KJV)

That quick temper you inherited, that road rage that surprises even you, that sharp tongue that cuts before you think—God says slow down. Anger isn't always wrong, but it's rarely quick and right at the same time. Being slow to anger doesn't mean being a pushover. It means being in control rather than controlled. That pause between trigger and response—that's where wisdom lives. Your kids need to see you angry about the right things in the right way.

Reflection Question: Where do you need to build in a pause between feeling and reacting?

DAY 43

"But God commendeth his love toward us, in that, while we were yet sinners, Christ died for us." — Romans 5:8 (KJV)

God loved you at your worst. Not after you cleaned up, not when you got your act together—while you were still a mess. That's the love you're called to show others. That family member who makes every gathering tense, that neighbor whose lifestyle offends you, that person whose politics make your blood boil—God loved you while you were unlovable. Now it's your turn to pass it on.

Reflection Question: Who in your life seems unlovable but needs to see God's love through you?

DAY 44

"And hath given to us the ministry of reconciliation." — 2 Corinthians 5:18 (KJV)

You're called to be a bridge builder, not a wall constructor. Reconciliation is your ministry—bringing together what's been torn apart. That relationship that seems irreparable? You serve a God who specializes in reconciliation. Maybe it's time to make the first move. Send the text, make the call, extend the invitation. Reconciliation doesn't mean everything goes back to how it was, but it means choosing peace over pride. Someone's waiting for you to take the first step.

Reflection Question: What broken relationship is God calling you to begin reconciling?

DAY 45

"Charity never faileth: but whether there be prophecies, they shall fail." —
1 Corinthians 13:8 (KJV)

Everything else has an expiration date except love. Your five-year plan might fail, your investments might tank, your health might decline—but love never fails. It's the only investment with guaranteed returns. When you don't know what to do, choose love. When you're not sure what to say, speak love. When everything else is falling apart, love is still working. It might not look like winning in the moment, but love always wins in the end.

Reflection Question: Where do you need to trust that love won't fail, even when everything else seems to be?

DAY 46

"There is no fear in love; but perfect love casteth out fear." — *1 John 4:18 (KJV)*

Fear and love can't coexist. When you're operating in fear—fear of rejection, failure, or loss—you're not operating in love. God's perfect love drives out those fears that keep you from fully living and loving. That risk you're afraid to take in your relationship, that vulnerability you're avoiding—fear is the enemy, not failure. God's love makes you bulletproof to rejection because you're already perfectly accepted. Let His love drive out the fears that are holding you back.

Reflection Question: What fear is keeping you from loving fully?

DAY 47

"Likewise, ye husbands, dwell with them according to knowledge, giving honour unto the wife." — 1 Peter 3:7 (KJV)

Living with your wife "according to knowledge" means being a student of her. Not assuming you know, but continually learning. Her needs change, her dreams evolve, her love language might shift. Are you still studying? Honor isn't just opening doors—it's understanding her heart. It's knowing when she needs you to fix something and when she just needs you to listen. It's recognizing her strengths and covering her weaknesses without making her feel weak.

Reflection Question: What do you need to learn about your wife that you've been assuming you already know?

DAY 48

"Lo, children are an heritage of the Lord: and the fruit of the womb is his reward." — Psalm 127:3 (KJV)

Your kids aren't interruptions to your life—they're investments in eternity. Every bedtime story, every caught baseball, every hard conversation is building heritage. You're not just raising kids; you're raising future parents, spouses, and disciples. When work feels more important than another game of catch, remember what's temporary and what's eternal. Your kids won't remember every toy you bought them, but they'll remember whether you were present. Heritage isn't passed down through DNA—it's passed down through discipleship.

Reflection Question: What heritage are you building into your children beyond material provision?

DAY 49

"And above all things have fervent charity among yourselves: for charity shall cover the multitude of sins." — 1 Peter 4:8 (KJV)

Love doesn't expose—it covers. Not covering up sin, but covering with grace. Your spouse's weaknesses, your children's mistakes, your friend's failures—love throws a blanket of grace over them all. This doesn't mean ignoring issues, but addressing them with love that protects dignity while promoting growth. That story about your spouse that would get laughs at guys' night—love keeps it covered. That mistake your child made—love addresses it privately before defending them publicly.

Reflection Question: Whose failures do you need to cover with love instead of exposing?

DAY 50

"Greater love hath no man than this, that a man lay down his life for his friends." — John 15:13 (KJV)

Laying down your life isn't usually dramatic—it's daily. It's choosing their needs over your preferences, their success over your recognition. It's dying to self in a thousand small ways that add up to a life of love. That promotion that would mean less time with family, that hobby that's becoming an escape from responsibility, that pride that keeps you from apologizing—these are opportunities to lay down your life. Love is measured in sacrifice, not sentiment.

Reflection Question: What part of your life needs to be laid down for someone you love?

DAY 51

"But a certain Samaritan, as he journeyed, came where he was: and when he saw him, he had compassion on him." — Luke 10:33 (KJV)

The Samaritan stopped for someone who would have probably ignored him on a good day. Love crosses cultural, racial, and social boundaries. It sees need, not category. Your neighbor isn't just the guy next door—it's anyone within reach of your love. That person who's nothing like you, who votes differently, lives differently, believes differently—they're your neighbor. Love doesn't check qualifications before showing compassion. The Samaritan loved without expecting anything in return. That's the kind of love that changes the world.

Reflection Question: Who outside your usual circle needs to experience your neighborly love?

DAY 52

"Rejoiceth not in iniquity, but rejoiceth in the truth." — 1 Corinthians 13:6 (KJV)

Love doesn't celebrate when someone you don't like fails. That competitor who went bankrupt, that ex who's struggling—love doesn't find satisfaction in their suffering. Instead, love celebrates truth, even when truth is uncomfortable. When your child owns their mistake, when your spouse shares a hard truth, when a friend confesses a struggle—love rejoices that truth is winning. Truth and love aren't opposites; they're dance partners. One without the other limps.

Reflection Question: Where do you need to celebrate truth instead of someone else's failure?

DAY 53

"Charity suffereth long, and is kind." — 1 Corinthians 13:4 (KJV)

Love has a long fuse. That spouse who's still struggling with the same issue, that child who keeps making the same mistake, that friend who can't seem to get it together—love keeps showing up. Patience isn't passive; it's persistent love that refuses to give up. You want microwave transformation, but God often works in slow-cooker time. Your patience might be the safe space someone needs to finally change. Don't mistake their slow progress for no progress. Love sees potential and waits for it to bloom.

Reflection Question: Where is God calling you to demonstrate patient love?

DAY 54

"Charity envieth not; charity vaunteth not itself, is not puffed up." — 1 Corinthians 13:4 (KJV)

Love celebrates others' wins without keeping score. When your friend gets the promotion you wanted, when your brother's marriage seems easier—love rejoices instead of comparing. Envy is love's enemy because it makes everything a competition. Your journey is yours. Their blessing doesn't diminish your potential. Love is secure enough to celebrate someone else's victory while waiting for your own. When you genuinely celebrate others, you're declaring that God has enough blessing for everyone.

Reflection Question: Whose success do you need to celebrate instead of envying?

DAY 55

"Beareth all things, believeth all things, hopeth all things, endureth all things." — 1 Corinthians 13:7 (KJV)

Love gives the benefit of the doubt. When your spouse is distant, love assumes they're struggling, not straying. When your friend doesn't call back, love assumes they're overwhelmed, not avoiding. Love interprets through the lens of grace. This isn't naivety—it's choosing to believe the best until proven otherwise. That assumption you're making about someone's motives—what if you're wrong? Love chooses the most generous interpretation possible. It's how God sees you.

Reflection Question: About whom do you need to start believing the best instead of assuming the worst?

DAY 56

"My little children, let us not love in word, neither in tongue; but in deed and in truth." — 1 John 3:18 (KJV)

Talk is cheap; love is expensive. Your family doesn't need more "I love you's" without the actions to back them up. Love shows up, stays late, gets messy. It's in the oil changes, the dishes done without being asked, the phone put down when they're talking. That service project you keep meaning to join, that neighbor who needs help moving, that single mom whose car needs fixing—love rolls up its sleeves. Your hands preach louder sermons than your mouth ever could.

Reflection Question: How can you move your love from words to actions today?

DAY 57

"Nevertheless I have somewhat against thee, because thou hast left thy first love." — Revelation 2:4 (KJV)

Remember when following Jesus was exciting? When prayer felt like conversation, not obligation? When worship was passion, not routine? Somewhere between then and now, duty replaced delight. God notices when love becomes mechanical. Your first love is calling you back—not to emotional immaturity but to authentic affection. That enthusiasm you had as a new believer wasn't childish; it was pure. God wants your heart, not just your habits. Return to that place where love for Him drives everything else.

Reflection Question: What would it look like to return to your first love for God?

DAY 58

"Thou shalt love thy neighbour as thyself." — Matthew 22:39 (KJV)

The assumption here is that you love yourself—not in a narcissistic way, but with appropriate care. You feed yourself when hungry, rest when tired, seek help when sick. God says extend that same care to others. How do you want to be treated when you fail? When you're struggling? When you're difficult? That's your blueprint for loving others. The grace you give yourself after messing up—give that to others. The patience you want when you're learning—extend that to them.

Reflection Question: How would your relationships change if you loved others the way you want to be loved?

DAY 59

"Hereby perceive we the love of God, because he laid down his life for us: and we ought to lay down our lives for the brethren." — 1 John 3:16 (KJV)

Love is measured in what you're willing to sacrifice. Jesus set the bar with His life. You might not be called to physical death, but you're called to die to self. That's harder sometimes—dying daily to your preferences, pride, and plans. Your sacrifice might look like skipping golf to attend your daughter's recital, or choosing a job that pays less but gives you more family time. It might mean swallowing your pride and apologizing first. Love always costs something. If it doesn't, it might not be love.

Reflection Question: What sacrifice is love calling you to make?

LEAP DAY BONUS

"Beloved, let us love one another: for love is of God; and every one that loveth is born of God, and knoweth God." — 1 John 4:7 (KJV)

This extra day reminds us that love is overflow. When you know God, love isn't manufactured—it's natural. You love because He first loved you. It's not about trying harder but about receiving more of His love and letting it spill over. Today, on this bonus day that comes once every four years, take a leap of love. Do something unexpectedly loving. Send that message you've been crafting in your head. Make that gesture you've been planning. Give that gift you've been considering. Love extravagantly, just because you can.

Reflection Question: What leap of love is God inviting you to take today?

MARCH: STRENGTH AND COURAGE

DAY 60

"The Lord is my strength and my shield; my heart trusted in him, and I am helped." — Psalm 28:7 (KJV)

Your gym membership might build your biceps, but real strength comes from somewhere else. David knew this. The guy who killed a lion with his bare hands said God was his strength. Think about that next time you're flexing in the mirror. Life will put you in headlocks you can't muscle your way out of. That diagnosis that knocked the wind out of you. The pink slip nobody saw coming. Your teenager looking you dead in the eye and saying they hate you. These moments don't care about your deadlift numbers. But when you're flat on your back, God's strength doesn't depend on yours. He's strong when you've got nothing left.

Reflection Question: What situation has you trying to be strong when you need to let God be strong for you?

DAY 61

"And he came thither unto a cave, and lodged there; and, behold, the word of the Lord came to him." — 1 Kings 19:9 (KJV)

Elijah just called down fire from heaven, but here he is, hiding in a cave, wanting to die. Even prophets have bad days. Your cave might be your garage, your office after hours, or that parking lot where you sit before going home. God didn't scold Elijah for being in the cave. He met him there. Your lowest points aren't too low for God. He shows up in caves, in doubts, in the moments when you wonder if you've got what it takes. Sometimes the cave is where you hear Him clearest—away from the noise, the expectations, the performance. Even Superman had a fortress of solitude.

Reflection Question: What cave are you hiding in, and what might God be trying to tell you there?

DAY 62

"And he said unto him, If now I have found grace in thy sight, then shew me a sign." — Judges 6:17 (KJV)

Gideon needed proof. Multiple times. The angel called him a mighty warrior while he was hiding in a winepress, threshing wheat like a scared kid. Sound familiar? God calling you something you don't feel? Here's the beautiful part: God gave him the signs. Every fleece, every test, God patiently proved Himself. Your doubts don't disqualify you. That business you're scared to start, that leadership role you don't feel ready for— God's patient with your need for confirmation. He'd rather have you moving forward uncertain than standing still in false confidence.

Reflection Question: What fleece do you need to put out, and what's keeping you from asking God for confirmation?

DAY 63

"Strengthen ye the weak hands, and confirm the feeble knees." — Isaiah 35:3 (KJV)

Your knees are allowed to shake. Isaiah isn't talking to warriors; he's talking to people whose knees are already weak. God doesn't recruit the already strong—He strengthens the weak who show up. Remember your first day as a dad? Your hands shook holding that tiny human. First time leading a meeting? Your voice probably cracked. That's not weakness; that's humanity. God specializes in steady hands and firm knees, but only after you admit they're shaking. The bravest thing you can do today might be showing up with shaking knees.

Reflection Question: Where do you need to show up even though your knees are shaking?

DAY 64

"I will not let thee go, except thou bless me." — Genesis 32:26 (KJV)

Jacob wrestled with God all night. Not prayed, not meditated—wrestled. Sometimes faith is a contact sport. You ever been there? Three AM, can't sleep, fighting God about something He's asking you to do or let go of? Jacob walked away with a limp and a blessing. Your spiritual limp might be that humility you gained from failure, that compassion born from your own struggles. Wrestling with God changes your walk. You might not win the match, but you'll win something better—a deeper connection with the One you're wrestling.

Reflection Question: What are you wrestling with God about, and what blessing might be hidden in the struggle?

DAY 65

"Now when Daniel knew that the writing was signed, he went into his house...and prayed...as he did aforetime." — Daniel 6:10 (KJV)

Daniel knew the decree. Pray and die. His response? Open the windows wider. That's courage—not the absence of consequences but the presence of conviction. He didn't pray in secret suddenly; he kept his regular appointment with God. Your lion's den might be a workplace that mocks your faith or a family that doesn't understand your convictions. Daniel teaches us that consistency is courage. Keep praying when they're watching. Keep your integrity when it costs you. The lions might roar, but they can't bite without God's permission.

Reflection Question: Where are you tempted to hide your faith to avoid the lions?

DAY 66

"Yea, though I walk through the valley of the shadow of death, I will fear no evil." — Psalm 23:4 (KJV)

Notice David says "through," not "in." Valleys have exits. That depression you're walking through, that grief that feels permanent—it's a valley, not your new address. The shadow of death is scary, but shadows can't actually hurt you. Walking through means you're moving, even when it's dark. One foot, then another. You might not see the path, but the Shepherd does. He's got night vision when all you've got is fear. The rod and staff aren't just for comfort—they're for guidance when you can't see where you're stepping.

Reflection Question: What valley are you treating like a permanent residence instead of passing through?

DAY 67

"And there went out a champion out of the camp of the Philistines, named Goliath." — 1 Samuel 17:4 (KJV)

Everyone has a Goliath. Yours might wear a suit, carry a diagnosis, or live in your past. It shows up every morning, taunting you, reminding you of your size in comparison. The whole army of Israel saw Goliath's size. David saw God's. Your giant only looks unbeatable because you're using the wrong measuring stick. Stop measuring your strength against your problem. Start measuring your problem against God's track record. David didn't kill Goliath with superior weapons—he killed him with superior perspective.

Reflection Question: What giant have you been measuring against yourself instead of against God?

DAY 68

"Let us therefore come boldly unto the throne of grace." — Hebrews 4:16 (KJV)

Boldly. Not timidly, not apologetically—boldly. Like a kid who knows his dad loves him, running into the CEO's office without knocking. That's your access level to God's throne. But here you are, treating prayer like you're bothering Him. Bold prayers aren't disrespectful; they're relational. God can handle your honest questions, your raw emotions, your audacious requests. That thing you think is too big to ask for? That situation you think is too messy to bring up? Bring it boldly. The throne you're approaching is grace, not judgment.

Reflection Question: What bold prayer have you been too timid to pray?

DAY 69

"But if not, be it known unto thee, O king, that we will not serve thy gods."
— Daniel 3:18 (KJV)

"But if not." Three words that change everything. These teenagers said God could save them, but even if He didn't, they wouldn't bow. That's faith with a backup plan that isn't actually a backup plan—it's the same plan: trust God regardless. Your furnace might be bankruptcy, divorce, or cancer. You're believing God for the miracle, but what if He doesn't? These boys teach us that faith isn't about getting out of the fire—it's about Who's in the fire with you. Sometimes God delivers you from it; sometimes He delivers you through it.

Reflection Question: Can you say "but if not" and still trust God completely?

DAY 70

"And at midnight Paul and Silas prayed, and sang praises unto God." —
Acts 16:25 (KJV)

Backs bleeding, feet in stocks, maximum security prison. Their response? Karaoke night. That's not denial—that's defiance. Praising God when everything goes wrong is spiritual warfare. Your midnight might be right now. Bills you can't pay, marriage falling apart, health failing. Paul and Silas teach us that worship is a weapon. You might not feel like singing, but sometimes praise is a choice, not a feeling. Start humming. Start with one thing you're grateful for. Watch how praise picks the locks that problems can't.

Reflection Question: What would happen if you started praising in your prison?

DAY 71

"And ye shall compass the city, all ye men of war, and go round about the city once." — *Joshua 6:3 (KJV)*

Walk in circles for seven days, then yell. That was God's military strategy. Makes no sense. But Joshua didn't edit God's instructions to seem more logical. Sometimes obedience means looking foolish to everyone watching. Your Jericho might be a problem that won't budge. God's instruction might seem ridiculous—forgive them, give when you're broke, stay when everything says leave. The walls don't fall because the strategy makes sense; they fall because you obeyed even when it didn't.

Reflection Question: What seemingly illogical instruction from God have you been resisting?

DAY 72

"By faith Noah, being warned of God of things not seen as yet...prepared an ark." — *Hebrews 11:7 (KJV)*

Noah built a boat where it had never rained. Every day, neighbors laughed. Every plank was laid by faith, not sight. Your obedience might look crazy to everyone watching. That career change, that ministry you're starting, that stand you're taking—they think you're building a boat in the desert. But Noah heard something they didn't. When you've heard from God, their opinions become background noise. Keep hammering. The rain will vindicate your obedience. Until then, build what God told you to build, even if you're the only one who understands why.

Reflection Question: What has God told you to build that others don't understand?

DAY 73

"But the ship was now in the midst of the sea, tossed with waves: for the wind was contrary." — Matthew 14:24 (KJV)

The disciples were exactly where Jesus told them to be, and they were still in a storm. Following God doesn't mean smooth sailing. Sometimes He sends you straight into contrary winds to teach you something calm seas never could. Jesus came walking on the thing that threatened them. Your storm might be the very thing Jesus uses to show up in a way you've never seen Him before. That contrary wind in your face? It might be pushing you toward a miracle. Stop cursing the storm and start looking for Jesus in it.

Reflection Question: How might Jesus be approaching you through your current storm?

DAY 74

"If ye have faith as a grain of mustard seed, ye shall say unto this mountain, Remove hence." — Matthew 17:20 (KJV)

Jesus didn't say you need mountain-sized faith to move mountains. Mustard-seed faith will do. That's about the size of the period at the end of this sentence. Your faith doesn't have to be huge; it just has to be real. That mountain blocking your view—debt, addiction, broken relationship—you keep waiting for your faith to grow bigger. But Jesus says you've got enough faith right now. The question isn't faith's size but its application. Stop measuring your faith and start using it.

Reflection Question: What mountain do you have enough faith to speak to right now?

DAY 75

"But David said unto Saul, Thy servant kept his father's sheep, and there came a lion." — 1 Samuel 17:34 (KJV)

David's resume for fighting Goliath was sheepherding. But those lonely nights with sheep were actually warrior training. The lion and bear were pop quizzes preparing him for the final exam. Your current mundane responsibility might be God's training ground for your future purpose. Those small victories nobody saw—staying faithful in your marriage when tempted, choosing integrity when nobody was watching—these are building giant-killing faith. God's watching how you handle the sheep before He lets you face Goliath.

Reflection Question: How might your current "sheep" be preparing you for future giants?

DAY 76

"But my servant Caleb, because he had another spirit with him...him will I bring into the land." — Numbers 14:24 (KJV)

Caleb saw the same giants everyone else saw. The difference? His spirit. Ten spies saw problems; Caleb saw promises. Same facts, different faith. At 85, he was still asking for mountains to conquer. Your spirit determines your story. Those obstacles everyone says are impossible? Caleb's spirit says, "Give me that mountain." Age, circumstances, popular opinion—none of it matters when you have a different spirit. Be the one voice of faith in a room full of fear.

Reflection Question: Where do you need to have a different spirit than everyone around you?

DAY 77

"But God hath chosen the foolish things of the world to confound the wise."
— 1 Corinthians 1:27 (KJV)

God's roster is weird. Stuttering Moses, tiny David, doubting Thomas, denying Peter. If God only used the qualified, He'd have a short list. Your weakness might be exactly what qualifies you for God's use. That thing you think disqualifies you—your past, your lack of education, your personality quirks—might be exactly why God picked you. He loves making trophies out of what others throw away. Your weakness is God's opportunity to show off His strength.

Reflection Question: What weakness might God want to use as your greatest strength?

DAY 78

"Fear ye not, stand still, and see the salvation of the Lord." — Exodus 14:13
(KJV)

Sometimes the bravest thing you can do is nothing. Israel's instinct was to run or fight. God said stand still. That's hard for men. We're fixers, fighters, figure-it-outers. But some Red Seas only part when you stop trying to swim across. That situation you're trying to force, manipulate, or control—what if God's waiting for you to stand still? Not passive, but positioned. Not giving up, but giving over. Sometimes courage looks like action; sometimes it looks like active waiting.

Reflection Question: Where do you need to stop striving and stand still?

DAY 79

"And his armourbearer said unto him, Do all that is in thine heart...I am with thee." — *1 Samuel 14:7 (KJV)*

Jonathan's armor bearer followed him into a two-man assault against an entire garrison. That's loyalty. That's courage by association. Sometimes you're called to be the hero; sometimes you're called to support one. Being an armor bearer requires its own kind of courage—supporting someone else's vision, protecting someone else's calling. Your role might be making someone else successful. That's not second place; that's strategic placement. Who needs you to say, "I'm with you" today?

Reflection Question: Who needs you to be their armor bearer right now?

DAY 80

"And Joshua set up twelve stones in the midst of Jordan." — *Joshua 4:9 (KJV)*

Joshua built a memorial in the middle of the river—where nobody would see it unless the water stopped again. Some monuments are just between you and God. Not every victory needs to be posted, not every testimony needs an audience. Build your memorials anyway. That private victory over temptation, that fear you faced alone with God—stack those stones. They're not for others; they're for you to remember when the next impossible situation comes. Your private memorials become your personal faith fuel.

Reflection Question: What private victory needs a memorial that only you and God know about?

DAY 81

"David therefore departed thence, and escaped to the cave Adullam...and every one that was in distress...gathered themselves unto him." — *1 Samuel 22:1-2 (KJV)*

David's mighty men started as distressed, indebted misfits in a cave. Your current crew might not look like much either. But God specializes in turning cave dwellers into kingdom builders. The broken people around you might be mighty men in development. Don't despise small beginnings or messy people. That struggling friend, that imperfect small group, that startup ministry—caves are where movements begin. David turned outcasts into warriors by believing in them before they believed in themselves.

Reflection Question: What cave situation might God be using to build something mighty?

DAY 82

"And after him was Shamgar...which slew of the Philistines six hundred men with an ox goad." — *Judges 3:31 (KJV)*

Shamgar had a farming tool, not a weapon. But he used what he had. Your ox goad might be your truck, your grill, your garage—ordinary things that become extraordinary when surrendered to God. Stop waiting for the perfect resources. Shamgar could have said, "When I get a real sword, then I'll fight." Instead, he grabbed his work tool and went to war. God's not asking what you wish you had—He's asking what you'll do with what you've got.

Reflection Question: What ordinary tool in your life could God use for extraordinary purposes?

DAY 83

"And I arose in the night, I and some few men with me; neither told I any man what my God had put in my heart." — Nehemiah 2:12 (KJV)

Nehemiah surveyed the broken walls at night, alone, before telling anyone his plan. Some visions need to be protected before they're proclaimed. Not everyone needs to know what God's stirring in your heart—yet. That business idea, that ministry vision, that life change you're contemplating—maybe it needs more midnight surveying before daylight announcing. Guard what God's growing in you. Not everyone who asks about your plans deserves to hear them.

Reflection Question: What has God put in your heart that needs protecting before proclaiming?

DAY 84

"He teacheth my hands to war, and my fingers to fight." — Psalm 144:1 (KJV)

God's not training you for comfort; He's training you for combat. Every trial is target practice. Every obstacle is an opportunity to learn heaven's warfare. You're not just surviving; you're training. The battles you face aren't random. They're specific training for your specific calling. That conflict at work, that spiritual warfare in your home—you're learning to fight with heaven's weapons. God's making a warrior out of you, one battle at a time.

Reflection Question: What is your current battle teaching you about spiritual warfare?

DAY 85

"Have not I commanded thee? Be strong and of a good courage; be not afraid." — Joshua 1:9 (KJV)

Three times God told Joshua to be courageous. Once should have been enough, right? But God knows we need reminders. Joshua was following Moses—talk about impossible shoes to fill. You might be in shoes that feel too big too. Courage isn't a feeling; it's a choice. God commands it, which means it's possible. That leadership role you're stepping into, that responsibility that terrifies you—God wouldn't command courage if He wasn't going to supply it.

Reflection Question: Where do you need to choose courage even though you don't feel it?

DAY 86

"Lord, it is nothing with thee to help, whether with many, or with them that have no power." — 2 Chronicles 14:11 (KJV)

Asa was outnumbered and admitted it. His prayer wasn't pretending to be strong—it was acknowledging he wasn't. God doesn't need your strength; He needs your surrender. The odds against you are irrelevant when God's with you. Your outnumbered situation—bills versus income, problems versus solutions—these ratios don't matter to God. Asa teaches us that honest prayers about our weakness move God more than fake claims of strength.

Reflection Question: Where do you need to admit you're outnumbered and invite God into the odds?

DAY 87

"And when they began to sing and to praise, the Lord set ambushments." —
2 Chronicles 20:22 (KJV)

Jehoshaphat put the worship team on the front lines. Singers before soldiers. That's either brilliant or insane. When three armies came against him, his battle strategy was a concert. Worship confuses the enemy more than weapons. Your battle might need more praise than planning. That situation that has you strategizing endlessly—what if you worshiped instead? The enemy expects fear, anger, retaliation. He doesn't know what to do with worship. Make your battlefield a worship service.

Reflection Question: What battle needs less strategy and more songs?

DAY 88

"And the Lord said unto Gideon, The people that are with thee are too many." — *Judges 7:2 (KJV)*

God cut Gideon's army from 32,000 to 300. Too many people would steal God's glory. Sometimes God reduces your resources so you'll rely on His power. That support system that disappeared, that opportunity that closed—maybe God's setting up a miracle. Less is more when God's involved. Your 300 might be all God needs. Stop counting what you don't have and start consecrating what you do. Gideon's 300 with God beat 135,000 without Him.

Reflection Question: Where might God be reducing your resources to increase your reliance?

DAY 89

"And she said, The Philistines be upon thee, Samson. And he awoke out of his sleep, and said, I will go out as at other times." — Judges 16:20 (KJV)

Samson didn't know his strength was gone. It didn't leave all at once—it leaked out through compromise. That's how strength usually goes, not in dramatic exits but in slow leaks. Small compromises, little surrenders, tiny betrayals of your convictions. Check your strength levels. That temptation that used to be easy to resist but isn't anymore—that's a leak. That spiritual discipline you've been neglecting—that's a leak. Samson's story warns us: you can lose your strength and not know it until you need it.

Reflection Question: Where might your strength be slowly leaking through compromise?

DAY 90

"That I may know him, and the power of his resurrection." — Philippians 3:10 (KJV)

Resurrection power isn't just for Easter Sunday. It's for your Monday morning, your marriage, your mistakes. The same power that raised Jesus from the dead lives in you. Not visiting, not occasionally available—living in you. Stop acting like you're operating on battery power when you're plugged into resurrection. That dead dream, that flatlined relationship, that buried hope—resurrection power specializes in dead things. But you have to believe it's there and act like it's real.

Reflection Question: What dead area of your life needs resurrection power applied to it?

April: Faith and Trust

Day 91

"If ye have faith as a grain of mustard seed, ye shall say unto this mountain, Remove hence." — Matthew 17:20 (KJV)

Ever held a mustard seed? It's basically nothing. A speck. Jesus says that's all the faith you need. We're over here trying to manufacture mountain-sized faith when God says pocket-lint faith will do. The power isn't in faith's size—it's in faith's object. You're staring at your mountain thinking your faith isn't big enough. Meanwhile, God's saying your speck of faith in Him is more powerful than perfect confidence in yourself. That whisper of belief you have? That counts. That tiny "maybe God can" thought? That's enough to start moving mountains.

Reflection Question: What would you attempt if you really believed your tiny faith was enough?

DAY 92

"Except I shall see in his hands the print of the nails...I will not believe." —
John 20:25 (KJV)

Thomas gets a bad rap. We call him "doubting Thomas" like his
honesty was weakness. But Jesus showed up specifically for
Thomas's doubt. He didn't kick him out of the group for needing proof. He gave him exactly what he needed. Your doubts
don't disqualify you; they position you for encounter. That
question you're afraid to ask, that proof you need—bring it to
Jesus. He can handle your honesty better than your fake faith.
Thomas touched the scars because he was honest about his
struggle.

*Reflection Question: What doubt do you need to honestly bring
to Jesus?*

DAY 93

*"Then Abraham fell upon his face, and laughed, and said in his heart, Shall
a child be born unto him that is an hundred years old?"* — *Genesis 17:17
(KJV)*

Abraham laughed at God's promise. The father of faith thought
God's plan was funny. And God still delivered. Your initial
reaction to God's promises doesn't determine their outcome.
That nervous laugh when God whispers something impossible? That's okay. God's not offended by your humanity.
Abraham's laughter didn't cancel the promise; it just made the
fulfillment sweeter. When Isaac (which means laughter) was
born, the joke was on doubt, not on God. Your impossible situation might be God's setup for the last laugh.

*Reflection Question: What promise from God seems so impos-
sible it makes you laugh?*

DAY 94

"But when he saw the wind boisterous, he was afraid; and beginning to sink, he cried, saying, Lord, save me." — *Matthew 14:30 (KJV)*

Peter gets criticized for sinking, but he's the only one who walked on water. Eleven guys stayed in the boat; one got wet trying. Better to sink attempting the impossible than stay dry discussing it. At least Peter knew what water-walking felt like, even if briefly. Your failed attempt at faith still beats someone else's successful safety. That business that failed, that risk that didn't pan out—you walked on water for a minute. Most people never leave the boat. And when Peter sank, Jesus caught him. That's all you need to know.

Reflection Question: What boat do you need to step out of, even if you might sink?

DAY 95

"And Abraham called the name of that place Jehovahjireh: as it is said to this day, In the mount of the Lord it shall be seen." — *Genesis 22:14 (KJV)*

Abraham named the place "The Lord Will Provide" after the provision, not before. He climbed that mountain with his son and a knife, not knowing how God would come through. The ram wasn't visible until the obedience was complete. Your provision might be hidden behind your obedience. That step God's asking you to take without showing you the safety net—the net appears after you jump, not before. Abraham teaches us that God's provision has perfect timing, but it's rarely early.

Reflection Question: What step of obedience are you delaying because you can't see the provision?

DAY 96

"And at midnight there was a cry made, Behold, the bridegroom cometh."
— Matthew 25:6 (KJV)

Five wise virgins had extra oil. Not because they were pessimistic, but because they were prepared. The difference between wise and foolish was margin. They all had lamps; only half had reserves. Your faith needs more than enough oil for normal—it needs reserves for midnight. When life goes into overtime, when the wait is longer than expected, do you have reserves? That extra time in the Word when things are good, that prayer life maintained in peaceful seasons—that's storing oil for midnight moments.

Reflection Question: Where do you need to build reserves before midnight comes?

DAY 97

"There is a lad here, which hath five barley loaves, and two small fishes: but what are they among so many?" — John 6:9 (KJV)

A kid's lunch fed thousands. But first, it had to be given. That boy could have kept his lunch, had a nice meal, and gone home full but unchanged. Instead, he gave what little he had and watched it become miraculous. Your "not enough" might be exactly what Jesus wants to multiply. That small amount of money, time, or talent you think won't make a difference—in Jesus' hands, it's more than enough. But you have to release it first. Miracles require giving God your lunch.

Reflection Question: What "small lunch" do you need to put in Jesus' hands?

DAY 98

"And they assayed to go into Bithynia: but the Spirit suffered them not." —
Acts 16:7 (KJV)

Paul wanted to go to Bithynia. God said no. Even apostles get
their plans redirected. That closed door you're banging on
might be God's protection, not His punishment. Paul's closed
door led to the Macedonian call—Europe got the gospel because Asia said no. Your rejection might be God's redirection.
That job you didn't get, that relationship that didn't work, that
opportunity that passed you by—what if God's got Macedonia
waiting because He blocked Bithynia? Trust the closed doors
as much as the open ones.

*Reflection Question: What closed door might actually be God's
protection or redirection?*

DAY 99

*"And the ravens brought him bread and flesh in the morning, and bread
and flesh in the evening."* — *1 Kings 17:6 (KJV)*

God used birds and a broke widow to provide for Elijah. Not
a king's treasury or a wealthy merchant—ravens and poverty.
God's provision rarely comes from logical sources. It comes
from unexpected places to remind you Who's really providing. That help you need might come from the last place you'd
expect. The person you think has nothing to offer, the opportunity that seems beneath you—God loves using unlikely
sources. Ravens don't typically share their food, and widows
don't usually have excess. But God's math is different.

*Reflection Question: What unlikely source might God be pre-
paring to provide through?*

DAY 100

"Wait on the Lord: be of good courage, and he shall strengthen thine heart: wait, I say, on the Lord." — Psalm 27:14 (KJV)

David said "wait" twice. Once wasn't enough because waiting is hard. We want microwave answers to slow-cooker prayers. But waiting isn't wasted time—it's weight training for faith. Every day you wait, you're building spiritual muscle. That answer you needed yesterday, that breakthrough that's overdue—the waiting is working something in you that the answer alone couldn't produce. God's not slow; He's thorough. Your wait is building a testimony that rushing would ruin.

Reflection Question: What is God developing in you through your current waiting season?

DAY 101

"Behold, I will put a fleece of wool in the floor; and if the dew be on the fleece only...then shall I know." — Judges 6:37 (KJV)

Gideon needed confirmation. Twice. With the same fleece. And God didn't rebuke him for it. Sometimes faith needs confirmation, and that's not weakness—it's wisdom. Gideon wasn't doubting God; he was confirming he heard right. That major decision you're facing—it's okay to ask for confirmation. Put out your fleece. Ask for clarity. God's not frustrated by your need for certainty when the stakes are high. He'd rather you be sure than sorry.

Reflection Question: What decision needs a fleece for confirmation?

DAY 102

"And when the cloud was taken up from the tabernacle, then after that the children of Israel journeyed." — *Numbers 9:17 (KJV)*

Israel moved when the cloud moved, stayed when it stayed. Sometimes for days, sometimes for months. They didn't control the schedule; they just followed the cloud. Your frustration might be that you're trying to make the cloud move on your timeline. That next season you're ready for—the cloud hasn't moved yet. That place you want to leave—the cloud's still hovering. Following God means moving at His pace, not yours. When the cloud moves, you'll know. Until then, set up camp.

Reflection Question: Are you trying to move without the cloud or stay when it's gone?

DAY 103

"Take therefore no thought for the morrow: for the morrow shall take thought for the things of itself." — *Matthew 6:34 (KJV)*

Jesus says stop borrowing tomorrow's troubles with today's faith. You're trying to solve next year's problems with today's grace. That's like trying to eat tomorrow's bread today—it doesn't exist yet. Your anxiety about the future is assuming God's grace won't show up. But grace arrives daily, like manna. Tomorrow's problems will come with tomorrow's provision. Today's grace is for today's troubles. Stop trying to live in two days at once.

Reflection Question: What tomorrow are you trying to solve with today's grace?

DAY 104

"Behold the fowls of the air: for they sow not, neither do they reap, nor gather into barns; yet your heavenly Father feedeth them." — Matthew 6:26 (KJV)

Birds don't have 401ks. They wake up trusting breakfast will be there. Jesus says you're worth more than birds, so why are you more worried? The sparrow outside your window is preaching a sermon about trust. This isn't about being irresponsible; it's about being unworried. Work hard, plan wisely, but don't let anxiety about provision steal today's peace. If God's feeding birds that can't plan ahead, He's got your mortgage covered.

Reflection Question: What are you worrying about that God's already handling?

DAY 105

"Notwithstanding, lest we should offend them, go thou to the sea, and cast an hook, and take up the fish that first cometh up." — Matthew 17:27 (KJV)

Tax money in a fish's mouth. That's not normal provision—that's God showing off. Peter could have worried about the tax, argued about its fairness, or panicked about payment. Instead, Jesus sent him fishing. The provision was swimming around, waiting to be caught. Your unexpected bill might have an unexpected answer. God's provision doesn't always come through overtime or side hustles. Sometimes it comes through obedience to seemingly unrelated instructions. Go fishing—your answer might be in the water.

Reflection Question: What unusual instruction might lead to your provision?

DAY 106

"For we walk by faith, not by sight." — *2 Corinthians 5:7 (KJV)*

Walking by faith is like driving at night. Your headlights only show 200 feet ahead, but that's enough to make the whole trip. You don't need to see the destination, just the next step. Faith is trusting God with the map while you focus on the road. Sight says, "Show me everything." Faith says, "Show me enough." That next step you're afraid to take because you can't see step ten—take it anyway. The path becomes visible as you walk, not before.

Reflection Question: What next step is faith asking you to take without seeing the whole path?

DAY 107

"Above all, taking the shield of faith, wherewith ye shall be able to quench all the fiery darts of the wicked." — *Ephesians 6:16 (KJV)*

Faith isn't just belief—it's a shield. It's defensive equipment against enemy attacks. Those thoughts that you're not enough, that God's forgotten you, that you've messed up too badly—those are darts. Faith blocks them. Your shield might feel heavy some days. That's because it's taking hits meant for your heart. Every doubt you reject, every fear you refuse, every lie you don't believe—that's your shield working. Keep holding it up. The arrows are real, but so is your shield.

Reflection Question: What fiery dart do you need to raise your shield against today?

DAY 108

"Now faith is the substance of things hoped for, the evidence of things not seen." — Hebrews 11:1 (KJV)

Faith makes invisible things real. It's not wishful thinking—it's spiritual sight. You're not pretending; you're perceiving what others can't see yet. Faith sees the business before it's built, the marriage before it's restored, the breakthrough before it happens. Your faith is evidence that what God promised exists, even if it's still invisible. Like a deed to property you haven't visited yet, faith is the paperwork proving ownership of promises still in transit.

Reflection Question: What invisible promise do you need to treat as already real?

DAY 109

"Through faith we understand that the worlds were framed by the word of God." — Hebrews 11:3 (KJV)

Everything you see started with words nobody could see. God spoke, and nothing became something. Your situation might need words of faith spoken over it. Not magic words, but faith words—declaring what God says despite what eyes see. That mess that looks permanent might just need faith words spoken over it. God framed worlds with words; you can frame your future with faith declarations. Speak what God says, not what circumstances show.

Reflection Question: What faith words need to be spoken over your situation?

DAY 110

"Even so faith, if it hath not works, is dead, being alone." — James 2:17 (KJV)

Faith without action is like a car without gas—it might look good, but it's not going anywhere. James isn't saying works save you; he's saying real faith moves. It doesn't just believe; it behaves. That thing you're believing God for—what action does faith require? Noah didn't just believe in rain; he built a boat. Your faith might need some lumber and nails. What you believe should affect what you do.

Reflection Question: What action does your faith need to take today?

DAY 111

"That in blessing I will bless thee, and in multiplying I will multiply thy seed as the stars of the heaven, and as the sand which is upon the sea shore." — Genesis 22:17 (KJV)

God promised Abraham descendants like sand. Ever tried counting sand? That's the point—it's impossible. God's promises for you are bigger than you can calculate. You're trying to count what God says is countless. Stop trying to figure out how God will do it. Abraham couldn't conceive how one son would become countless descendants. Your small beginning doesn't determine your big ending. God specializes in multiplication that doesn't make mathematical sense.

Reflection Question: What promise from God are you trying to calculate instead of trust?

DAY 112

"Trust in the Lord with all thine heart; and lean not unto thine own understanding." — Proverbs 3:5 (KJV)

Your understanding is a terrible walking stick. It'll break when you need it most. God says trust Me, not your ability to figure it out. That situation that makes no sense—it doesn't have to. Faith isn't understanding everything; it's trusting the One who does. Leaning on your understanding is exhausting. You weren't designed to carry the weight of figuring everything out. Let God be God. Trust Him with the outcomes you can't control and the answers you can't compute.

Reflection Question: Where are you leaning on understanding instead of trusting God?

DAY 113

"In whom we have boldness and access with confidence by the faith of him." — Ephesians 3:12 (KJV)

You have backstage passes to the throne room. Not because you earned them, but because Jesus gave you His credentials. That prayer you've been polishing, trying to make it perfect— just say it. You have access. Confidence isn't arrogance when it's based on Christ's credentials, not yours. You can walk into God's presence like you belong there, because through Jesus, you do. Stop standing at the door when you've been invited to the table.

Reflection Question: What do you need to confidently bring to God's throne?

DAY 114

"Knowing this, that the trying of your faith worketh patience." — James 1:3 (KJV)

Faith gets tested like gold gets refined—through fire. That trial isn't trying to break your faith; it's trying to prove it. Every test is producing something you'll need later: patience, endurance, character. Your faith test might feel like failure, but it's actually graduation prep. You don't test what you don't plan to use. God's testing your faith because He's got plans that require proven faith, not theoretical faith.

Reflection Question: How might your current test be preparing you for future purpose?

DAY 115

"But without faith it is impossible to please him: for he that cometh to God must believe that he is." — Hebrews 11:6 (KJV)

God's love language is faith. You can give, serve, and sacrifice, but without faith, you're speaking a language He doesn't respond to. Faith isn't just important—it's essential. It's the currency of the Kingdom. You're trying to impress God with your performance when He just wants your faith. Believe He is who He says He is. Believe He'll do what He says He'll do. That's what pleases Him—not your perfection, but your trust.

Reflection Question: Where have you been trying to please God with performance instead of faith?

DAY 116

"God hath dealt to every man the measure of faith." — *Romans 12:3 (KJV)*

You've been issued faith. It came standard with salvation. You're not faithless; you might just have your faith pointed in the wrong direction. That faith you have in failure—what if you redirected it toward God's faithfulness? Stop saying you don't have enough faith. God gave you a measure. It might be a teaspoon right now, but it's enough to start. Use what you have, and watch it grow. Faith is like a muscle—it grows with use, not wishing.

Reflection Question: How can you exercise the measure of faith you already have?

DAY 117

"Fight the good fight of faith, lay hold on eternal life." — *1 Timothy 6:12 (KJV)*

Faith is a fight, not a feeling. Some days you'll fight for every ounce of belief. That's not weakness—that's warfare. The enemy contests faith because he knows its power. If faith wasn't dangerous to darkness, he wouldn't fight it so hard. Your faith fight might look like choosing worship when you want to worry, declaring promises when problems are screaming, standing when everything says fall. Keep fighting. The fight itself is proof your faith matters.

Reflection Question: What faith fight do you need to engage in today?

DAY 118

"Looking unto Jesus the author and finisher of our faith." — Hebrews 12:2 (KJV)

Jesus started your faith story, and He'll finish it. You're not responsible for conjuring up faith or maintaining it alone. He who began this good work will complete it. Your job is to look at Him, not at your faith levels. Stop measuring your faith and start focusing on the Faithful One. He's both author and editor of your faith journey. The plot twists that scare you don't surprise Him. He knows how your story ends, and it's good.

Reflection Question: Where do you need to stop focusing on your faith and start focusing on Jesus?

DAY 119

"This is a faithful saying, and worthy of all acceptation, that Christ Jesus came into the world to save sinners." — 1 Timothy 1:15 (KJV)

Some things are faithful sayings—absolutely reliable, completely trustworthy. Christ came to save sinners. Period. Not former sinners, not moderate sinners—sinners. That includes you on your worst day. Your faith doesn't have to be perfect because His faithfulness is. He came for people who mess up, doubt, and fail. That's the faithful saying you can bank on. When your faith wavers, His faithfulness doesn't.

Reflection Question: What faithful saying do you need to lean on when your faith feels weak?

DAY 120

"And the apostles said unto the Lord, Increase our faith." — Luke 17:5 (KJV)

Even apostles needed more faith. They walked with Jesus and still said, "We need more." That prayer for increased faith isn't admission of failure—it's acknowledgment of need. God honors the honest request for more faith. Stop pretending your faith is sufficient. Ask for more. The disciples didn't get rebuked for this request; they got teaching about mustard seeds. Your prayer for more faith might be the most faith-filled prayer you can pray.

Reflection Question: Where do you need to honestly ask God to increase your faith?

MAY: PURPOSE AND CALLING

DAY 121

"Before I formed thee in the belly I knew thee; and before thou camest forth out of the womb I sanctified thee." — Jeremiah 1:5 (KJV)

You weren't an accident or afterthought. Before your parents even met, God had your number. That purpose you're searching for? It's not something you create—it's something you discover. God's already written it; you just need to read it. Think about that. The Creator of galaxies took time to think about you specifically. Your quirks, your strengths, even that thing you think disqualifies you—all part of the blueprint. You're not trying to become something; you're uncovering what you've always been meant to be.

Reflection Question: What if your biggest struggle is actually connected to your purpose?

DAY 122

"And who knoweth whether thou art come to the kingdom for such a time as this?" — Esther 4:14 (KJV)

Esther didn't want to be queen. She was hiding her identity, playing it safe. Then Mordecai drops this bomb: maybe you're here for this exact crisis. Your position isn't about comfort—it's about purpose. That job you stumbled into, that neighborhood you ended up in, that skill everyone always asks you about—these aren't random. You're positioned for something. Maybe that influence you've been downplaying is exactly what someone needs right now.

Reflection Question: What position has God given you that He might want to use right now?

DAY 123

"But Jonah rose up to flee unto Tarshish from the presence of the Lord." — Jonah 1:3 (KJV)

Jonah bought a ticket in the opposite direction from his calling. We judge him, then do the same thing with our credit cards and calendars. Running from purpose doesn't always look like rebellion—sometimes it looks like being really busy with good things that aren't God things. Here's what Jonah learned: you can run from your calling, but you'll end up in the belly of something. That restlessness you feel? Might be because you're on a boat to Tarshish when God called you to Nineveh.

Reflection Question: What Nineveh are you avoiding by staying busy with Tarshish?

DAY 124

"And he said, Who art thou, Lord? And the Lord said, I am Jesus whom thou persecutest." — Acts 9:5 (KJV)

Paul was crushing it in his career—rising star, perfect resume, clear trajectory. Then Jesus knocked him off his horse and gave him a completely different mission. Sometimes God disrupts your plans because He has better ones. That career disruption, that unexpected turn—what if it's not a detour but a Damascus road? Paul thought he was serving God one way; turns out God had something entirely different in mind. Your disruption might be your new direction.

Reflection Question: What disruption in your life might actually be God redirecting your purpose?

DAY 125

"Come now therefore, and I will send thee unto Pharaoh." — Exodus 3:10 (KJV)

Moses was 80 when God called him to his life's main purpose. Eighty. He'd already had two careers—prince and shepherd. If you think you've missed your window, think again. God's timing would fail every human resources department. You're not too old, and it's not too late. Moses thought his revolutionary days ended when he fled Egypt at 40. Turns out that was just preparation. Your past wasn't wasted; it was training. Everything you've done has prepared you for what's next.

Reflection Question: What past experience might God be ready to use for future purpose?

DAY 126

"Then Samuel took the horn of oil, and anointed him in the midst of his brethren." — *1 Samuel 16:13 (KJV)*

David got anointed king, then went back to watching sheep. The crown didn't come with the oil. Between your calling and your throne, there's usually a field. You might be anointed for something you're not positioned for yet. That gap between promise and position? That's where character gets built. David learned to fight bears before he faced giants, to lead sheep before he led armies. Your current obscurity might be preparing you for future opportunity.

Reflection Question: What are you learning in your field that you'll need for your throne?

DAY 127

"But ye are a chosen generation, a royal priesthood, an holy nation, a peculiar people." — *1 Peter 2:9 (KJV)*

Peculiar isn't an insult—it's your identity. You're supposed to be different. That thing about you that doesn't fit the mold? That might be exactly what God wants to use. Stop trying to be normal when God made you peculiar. Your coworkers think you're weird for your priorities. Your family doesn't get your faith. Good. You're not called to blend in; you're called to stand out. Salt doesn't work if it tastes like everything else.

Reflection Question: What peculiar thing about you have you been trying to normalize?

DAY 128

"And Jesus said unto them, Come ye after me, and I will make you to become fishers of men." — Mark 1:17 (KJV)

Jesus didn't ask fishermen to become shepherds. He transformed what they already were. "You catch fish? Great, let's use that skill for people." Your calling might not require a career change—just a perspective shift. That thing you're naturally good at—selling, building, teaching, fixing—God wants to baptize it for Kingdom purposes. Peter didn't stop being a fisherman; he just fished for something eternal. Your skill set is your ministry toolkit.

Reflection Question: How could God use your current skills for Kingdom purposes?

DAY 129

"And Joseph dreamed a dream, and he told it his brethren: and they hated him yet the more." — Genesis 37:5 (KJV)

Joseph's dreams got him thrown in a pit. Your vision might not get standing ovations either. Sometimes God gives you a glimpse of your future that nobody else can see or appreciate. Their lack of enthusiasm doesn't invalidate your vision. Between dream and destiny, Joseph hit multiple pits—literal and figurative. But every pit was positioning him for the palace. Your dream might take you through some dark places before it takes you to your destination.

Reflection Question: What dream has God given you that others don't understand?

DAY 130

"And because he was of the same craft, he abode with them, and wrought: for by their occupation they were tentmakers." — Acts 18:3 (KJV)

Paul changed the world while making tents. His day job funded his purpose. Not everyone's calling comes with a salary. Sometimes you work to eat and minister to live. There's no shame in the side hustle that funds the kingdom hustle. Your 9-to-5 might be the platform for your calling, not a distraction from it. Paul made tents and disciples. Your cubicle might be your mission field, your workplace your congregation. Ministry doesn't always look ministerial.

Reflection Question: How might your day job be the vehicle for your calling?

DAY 131

"And the angel of the Lord spake unto Philip, saying, Arise, and go toward the south." — Acts 8:26 (KJV)

Philip was crushing it in Samaria—crowds, miracles, revival. Then God said, "Leave and go to the desert." One Ethiopian eunuch was waiting there. Philip left the masses for one man. Sometimes purpose looks like interruption. That detour God's asking you to take, that one person who needs your time—that might be the whole point. Philip's willingness to leave the revival for the desert changed a nation. Ethiopia got the gospel because Philip valued obedience over opportunity.

Reflection Question: What interruption might actually be your divine appointment?

DAY 132

"And he said, Thy name shall be called no more Jacob, but Israel." —
Genesis 32:28 (KJV)

Jacob wrestled all night and walked away with a new name
and a limp. Sometimes discovering your purpose is a fight. You
might walk differently afterward, but you'll know who you really are. That internal wrestling match about your calling—it's
not lack of faith. Jacob had to wrestle to become Israel. Your
struggle with purpose might be the very thing that reveals it.
Some answers only come through wrestling.

*Reflection Question: What are you wrestling with God about
regarding your purpose?*

DAY 133

"He saith unto him the third time, Simon, son of Jonas, lovest thou me?" —
John 21:17 (KJV)

Peter denied Jesus three times. Jesus restored him three
times. Your failure doesn't disqualify you from purpose. It
might actually qualify you to help others who fail the same
way. Peter's denial became part of his testimony, not the end
of it. Jesus didn't find a replacement apostle. He restored the
broken one. Your biggest failure might become your greatest
ministry. The thing you're most ashamed of might be the very
experience someone needs to hear about.

*Reflection Question: How might God want to use your biggest
failure for His purpose?*

DAY 134

"And the angel of the Lord appeared unto him in a flame of fire out of the midst of a bush." — Exodus 3:2 (KJV)

Moses was doing his regular shepherd routine when a bush caught fire and didn't burn up. Your calling might interrupt your common. God speaks through burning bushes—ordinary things made extraordinary by His presence. Turn aside and look. That unusual thing happening in your ordinary life—pay attention. Moses could have kept walking, decided it was just desert heat playing tricks. Your burning bush might be disguised as a normal day with an unusual moment.

Reflection Question: What "burning bush" moment have you been walking past?

DAY 135

"And I have filled him with the spirit of God, in wisdom, and in understanding, and in knowledge, and in all manner of workmanship." — Exodus 31:3 (KJV)

Bezaleel's calling was craftmanship. God filled him with the Spirit to build stuff. Not to preach, prophecy, or perform miracles—to work with his hands. Your calling might be more practical than you think. That skill people always compliment—woodworking, coding, organizing, cooking—that might be your ministry. God needs builders as much as preachers. Bezaleel built the physical space where God's presence dwelt. What are you supposed to build?

Reflection Question: What practical skill might be your spiritual calling?

DAY 136

"He that is faithful in that which is least is faithful also in much." — Luke 16:10 (KJV)

You want the big assignment, but you're phoning in the small one. God's watching how you handle the little before He hands you the much. That entry-level position, that small ministry, that handful of people—this is your proving ground. David was faithful with sheep before he got people. Joseph was faithful in prison before the palace. Your current "least" is audition for your future "much." How you handle today determines what you're handed tomorrow.

Reflection Question: What "little" thing needs your faithfulness right now?

DAY 137

"And Elisha said, I pray thee, let a double portion of thy spirit be upon me." — 2 Kings 2:9 (KJV)

Elisha didn't want Elijah's ministry—he wanted double. He wasn't content to maintain; he wanted to multiply. Your spiritual father's ceiling should be your floor. God's not looking for copies but for those who'll go further. You're not meant to repeat the last generation's accomplishments but to build on them. Elisha did twice as many miracles as Elijah. What if God wants to do more through you than through those you're following?

Reflection Question: Whose mantle are you meant to pick up and double?

DAY 138

"Let no man despise thy youth; but be thou an example of the believers." —
1 Timothy 4:12 (KJV)

Timothy was young and insecure. Paul said lead anyway. Your age doesn't disqualify you—whether you think you're too young or too old. God's not checking your birth certificate; He's checking your availability. Stop waiting for more years, more experience, more credibility. Timothy led churches while others his age were still finding themselves. If God's calling you, your age is irrelevant. He qualifies the called, regardless of their graduation date.

Reflection Question: How is your age becoming an excuse for not pursuing your calling?

DAY 139

"Thy prayers and thine alms are come up for a memorial before God." —
Acts 10:4 (KJV)

Cornelius wasn't even saved yet, but his prayers got heaven's attention. He was searching, and God sent Peter. Your seeking matters. That prayer you think doesn't count because you're not sure you're doing it right—God's listening. Sometimes purpose begins with prayer before you even know what you're praying for. Cornelius's purpose was to open the gospel to Gentiles, but it started with him just praying as best he knew how. Start where you are.

Reflection Question: What prayer is God using to reveal your purpose?

DAY 140

"And David said unto him, Fear not: for I will surely shew thee kindness for Jonathan thy father's sake." — *2 Samuel 9:7 (KJV)*

Mephibosheth was hiding, crippled, forgotten. David brought him to the royal table. He didn't earn it, deserve it, or expect it. Sometimes purpose isn't about what you do but about whose table you're invited to. You might feel like Mephibosheth— damaged, disqualified, forgotten. But God's got a seat at His table with your name on it. Your limitations don't limit your purpose. Mephibosheth ate at the king's table for the rest of his life.

Reflection Question: What table is God inviting you to despite your limitations?

DAY 141

"Fear not: for I have redeemed thee, I have called thee by thy name; thou art mine." — *Isaiah 43:1 (KJV)*

God doesn't do mass mailings. He calls by name. Your purpose isn't generic; it's got your name on it. That thing only you can do the way you do it—that's not coincidence; that's calling. You're not one of many; you're specifically chosen. God knew your name before your parents picked it. Your calling is as unique as your fingerprint. Stop trying to fulfill someone else's purpose when yours is waiting.

Reflection Question: What calling has your specific name on it?

DAY 142

"As my Father hath sent me, even so send I you." — John 20:21 (KJV)

You're not just saved; you're sent. Jesus didn't rescue you to bench you but to deploy you. The same intentionality with which the Father sent Jesus, Jesus sends you. You're on mission, not vacation. Where has He sent you? Maybe it's not Africa or Asia—maybe it's accounting or athletics. Your sent place might be your workplace, your gym, your neighborhood. You're a missionary; you just might not need a passport.

Reflection Question: Where has Jesus sent you that you've been treating as coincidence?

DAY 143

"Which in time past was to thee unprofitable, but now profitable to thee and to me." — Philemon 1:11 (KJV)

Onesimus went from runaway slave to profitable servant. His name meant "profitable," but he lived unprofitably until he met Paul. Sometimes discovering purpose requires someone else to see it in you first. Your past unprofitability doesn't determine your future usefulness. Onesimus's story changed when someone believed in his potential. Who needs you to be their Paul? Who's your Paul, seeing profit where you see problems?

Reflection Question: What "unprofitable" part of your life is God making profitable?

DAY 144

"And they said unto me, The remnant that are left...are in great affliction and reproach: the wall of Jerusalem also is broken down." — Nehemiah 1:3 (KJV)

Nehemiah had a good job, comfortable life, secure position. Then he heard about broken walls and couldn't sleep. Your burden might be your calling. That problem that bothers you more than it bothers others—pay attention. He was cup-bearer to the king, not a contractor. But the burden qualified him more than expertise. Sometimes God doesn't call the equipped; He equips the burdened. What breaks your heart might be what you're meant to build.

Reflection Question: What burden won't leave you alone that might be your calling?

DAY 145

"Likewise also was not Rahab the harlot justified by works, when she had received the messengers?" — James 2:25 (KJV)

Rahab went from prostitute to the lineage of Jesus. Her past didn't disqualify her from purpose. She's in the Hall of Faith with a résumé that would fail most background checks. Grace writes better stories than karma. Your history doesn't have to be your destiny. Rahab's profession didn't define her purpose. She hid spies and changed history. God's not looking at your past; He's looking at your potential.

Reflection Question: What past is God wanting to transform into purpose?

DAY 146

"And there came a certain poor widow, and she threw in two mites." —
Mark 12:42 (KJV)

Her offering was pocket change, but Jesus called the disciples over to watch. She didn't know she was teaching a lesson that would last millennia. Your small contribution might be someone's life-changing encounter. Purpose isn't always big and flashy. Sometimes it's two mites that nobody notices except Jesus. That small act of faithfulness, that quiet service, that unnoticed sacrifice—heaven's taking notes. Small obedience can have eternal impact.

Reflection Question: What small act of purpose are you undervaluing?

DAY 147

"And as they came out, they found a man of Cyrene, Simon by name: him they compelled to bear his cross." — Matthew 27:32 (KJV)

Simon was just coming in from the country, wrong place at the wrong time—or was it? He carried the cross of Christ. Sometimes your purpose finds you when you're just passing through. That interruption might be your intersection with destiny. He didn't volunteer; he was compelled. But he literally helped Jesus carry the cross. Your reluctant yes to an unexpected assignment might be more significant than you realize. Some purposes choose you.

Reflection Question: What unexpected burden might actually be a holy purpose?

DAY 148

"And in the fourth watch of the night Jesus went unto them, walking on the sea." — Matthew 14:25 (KJV)

The fourth watch is 3-6 AM—the darkest, hardest part of night. That's when Jesus showed up walking on water. Your purpose might become clearest in your darkest hour. Don't quit in the third watch. The disciples had been rowing all night, getting nowhere. Then Jesus came doing the impossible. Your exhausting effort might be setting the stage for supernatural intervention. Purpose often arrives in the fourth watch.

Reflection Question: What fourth watch are you in where purpose might be approaching?

DAY 149

"And the Lord said unto him, Arise, and go into the street which is called Straight." — Acts 9:11 (KJV)

Ananias was told to go pray for Saul—the guy killing Christians. His purpose was to help his enemy become an apostle. Sometimes God calls you to bless the very person you'd rather avoid. Ananias could have said no. Saul would have stayed blind, and we might not have half the New Testament. Your willingness to help someone you don't like might impact generations. Purpose doesn't always feel safe.

Reflection Question: Who is God asking you to help that you'd rather avoid?

DAY 150

"And found a certain Jew named Aquila...with his wife Priscilla...and because he was of the same craft, he abode with them." — Acts 18:2-3 (KJV)

A married couple who made tents and disciples. They're always mentioned together, purpose partners. Their home was a church, their business a ministry platform. Sometimes purpose is a team sport. They discipled Apollos, hosted Paul, risked their necks for the gospel. No spotlight ministry, just steady faithfulness. Your purpose might be supporting someone else's purpose. Not everyone's meant to be Paul; someone needs to be Aquila and Priscilla.

Reflection Question: Whose purpose are you meant to support with yours?

DAY 151

"This woman was full of good works and almsdeeds which she did." — Acts 9:36 (KJV)

Dorcas made clothes for widows. That was her ministry. When she died, they didn't talk about her sermons but showed Peter the coats she made. Her needle was her ministry tool. Purpose can be practical. God raised her from the dead. He doesn't resurrect everyone, but He brought back the seamstress. What you think is too ordinary to be ministry might be exactly what your community needs. Your purpose might be meeting practical needs with Kingdom love.

Reflection Question: What practical skill is your underestimated purpose?

June: God's Provision and Faithfulness

Day 152

"And the oil stayed." — *2 Kings 4:6 (KJV)*

The widow's oil kept pouring until she ran out of jars. God's provision matched her preparation. She could have gathered two jars or two hundred—the oil would have kept flowing. Sometimes the limit isn't God's supply but our capacity to receive. Think about that. She determined how much miracle she got by how many vessels she gathered. Your preparation level might be determining your provision level. God's ready to pour, but do you have enough jars?

Reflection Question: Where might small thinking be limiting God's provision?

DAY 153

"There is a lad here, which hath five barley loaves, and two small fishes: but what are they among so many?" — John 6:9 (KJV)

A kid's lunch became a buffet for thousands. But first, it had to be handed over. That insufficient resource you're holding—what if it's exactly what Jesus wants to multiply? Your "not enough" plus Jesus equals more than enough. The disciples saw impossibility. The boy saw opportunity. Everyone ate because one kid didn't keep his lunch to himself. Your small offering might be someone else's miracle meal.

Reflection Question: What "small lunch" do you need to put in Jesus' hands?

DAY 154

"And when the dew that lay was gone up, behold, upon the face of the wilderness there lay a small round thing." — Exodus 16:14 (KJV)

Every morning, fresh bread on the ground. But it came with rules: gather daily, don't hoard. Friday, get double. God's provision came with instructions about trust. He wanted daily dependence, not stockpiled security. You want next month's provision today. God provides daily bread because He wants daily relationship. That manna you're trying to store is going to rot. Tomorrow's provision comes with tomorrow's sunrise.

Reflection Question: Where are you trying to stockpile what God wants to provide daily?

DAY 155

"And it shall be, that thou shalt drink of the brook; and I have commanded the ravens to feed thee there." — *1 Kings 17:4 (KJV)*

God sent Elijah to a brook with a catering service of ravens. Not a river—a brook that would dry up. Not eagles—ravens, unclean birds. God's provision rarely looks like we expect. Your brook might seem insufficient, your ravens might seem wrong. But God's provision doesn't follow human logic. That unusual source of help, that temporary solution—maybe that's exactly what God ordered.

Reflection Question: What unexpected provision are you rejecting because it doesn't look right?

DAY 156

"And she said, As the Lord thy God liveth, I have not a cake, but an handful of meal in a barrel." — *1 Kings 17:12 (KJV)*

She was preparing her last meal, planning to die. Elijah said make him a cake first. That's audacious—or prophetic. Her obedience to feed the prophet first meant her meal barrel never emptied. Sometimes provision requires putting God first when you barely have enough for yourself. That tithe when money's tight, that service when time's scarce—God multiplies what we prioritize for Him.

Reflection Question: What "last meal" does God want you to share first?

DAY 157

"Behold, I will stand before thee there upon the rock in Horeb; and thou shalt smite the rock." — Exodus 17:6 (KJV)

Water from a rock. That's not how wells work. But Israel was thirsty, and God told Moses to hit a rock with a stick. Your provision might require you to do something that seems ridiculous. The rock had water in it the whole time—it just needed to be accessed God's way. Your provision might already be present, just waiting for obedience to release it.

Reflection Question: What "rock" might God be telling you to strike for provision?

DAY 158

"So I prophesied as I was commanded: and as I prophesied, there was a noise." — Ezekiel 37:7 (KJV)

Ezekiel spoke to skeletons and they became an army. But he had to prophesy to bones—talk to dead things like they could hear. Your situation might need you to speak life where you see death. Those dead dreams, that flatlined relationship, that buried hope—what if they're just waiting for a word? Ezekiel didn't analyze the bones; he prophesied to them. Sometimes faith speaks to what is not as though it were.

Reflection Question: What "dry bones" need you to prophesy life over them?

DAY 159

"Let us make a little chamber, I pray thee, on the wall; and let us set for him there a bed." — 2 Kings 4:10 (KJV)

She built a prophet's room and got a promised son. Her hospitality investment yielded a miracle return. She wasn't trying to get something—she was trying to give something. But giving positions you for receiving. That space you could share, that resource you could offer, that table you could open—your provision for others might trigger God's provision for you. The Shunammite woman discovered that making room for God's servant made room for God's miracle.

Reflection Question: What room can you make that might make room for miracles?

DAY 160

"The barrel of meal wasted not, neither did the cruse of oil fail." — 1 Kings 17:16 (KJV)

It never ran out, but it never overflowed either. Just enough, every day, for over two years. Sometimes God's provision isn't abundant—it's sufficient. And sufficient that never fails is better than abundance that does. You want overflow; God provides enough. But His enough is always enough. The widow's barrel teaches us that consistent sufficient beats sporadic abundance.

Reflection Question: Where do you need to be grateful for sufficient instead of waiting for abundance?

DAY 161

"Notwithstanding, lest we should offend them, go thou to the sea, and cast an hook." — Matthew 17:27 (KJV)

Tax money in a fish's mouth. Peter didn't find it—he caught it. The provision was swimming around, waiting to be caught. Your answer might not be sitting still; it might be in motion. Jesus could have materialized money. Instead, He sent Peter fishing. Sometimes provision requires participation. Your miracle might have a hook requirement.

Reflection Question: What action might hook your swimming provision?

DAY 162

"And, behold, an angel touched him, and said unto him, Arise and eat." — 1 Kings 19:5 (KJV)

Elijah was suicidal, exhausted, done. God's response? A nap and a snack. Not a sermon, not a scolding—sleep and food. Sometimes the most spiritual thing is the most practical. That heavenly cake gave Elijah strength for forty days. One meal from heaven sustained a journey. Your provision might not be daily; it might be one powerful deposit that carries you through a season.

Reflection Question: What practical provision are you spiritualizing when you just need to receive it?

DAY 163

"Thou preparest a table before me in the presence of mine enemies." —
Psalm 23:5 (KJV)

Not a hiding place, not an escape route—a table. In front of
your enemies. God's provision doesn't always remove you from
problems; sometimes it feeds you in front of them. That provision coming while problems persist—that's the table. Your
enemies have to watch you eat. Your crisis becomes the back-
drop for God's catering service.

*Reflection Question: What table is God preparing that your
enemies have to watch?*

DAY 164

*"But they that wait upon the Lord shall renew their strength; they shall
mount up with wings as eagles."* — *Isaiah 40:31 (KJV)*

Eagles don't flap frantically—they catch thermals and soar.
The wind does the work. Your strength renewal might not be
about trying harder but about catching what God's already
providing. Waiting on God isn't passive—it's positioning. Eagles
wait for the right wind. Your provision might be waiting for
you to stop flapping and start waiting.

*Reflection Question: Where do you need to stop flapping and
start soaring?*

DAY 165

"Thy shoes are not waxen old upon thy feet." — Deuteronomy 29:5 (KJV)

Forty years, same shoes. They didn't get new ones—the old ones didn't wear out. Sometimes God's provision is preservation, not replacement. What you have lasting longer than it should—that's provision too. That car that should have died, that appliance still working, that job that hasn't ended—God's provision includes supernatural preservation. Not everything needs to be new to be miraculous.

Reflection Question: What preservation miracle are you overlooking while waiting for provision?

DAY 166

"And the Lord went before them by day in a pillar of a cloud...and by night in a pillar of fire." — Exodus 13:21 (KJV)

Shade in the desert sun, light in the desert night. God's provision matched the need. The cloud was useless at night; the fire unnecessary during day. His provision is specific to your situation. Stop asking for fire when you need cloud. That provision that worked for someone else might not be what you need. God's got situation-specific supply for your particular desert.

Reflection Question: Are you asking for someone else's provision instead of what you actually need?

DAY 167

"And there went forth a wind from the Lord, and brought quails from the sea." — Numbers 11:31 (KJV)

They complained about manna, so God sent meat. The wind brought quail three feet deep. Be careful what you complain for—God might give it to you. Sometimes the provision you demand isn't the provision you need. Israel got meat but also plague. Their complaining brought provision with problems. God's first provision (manna) was better than their demanded provision (quail). Trust His menu.

Reflection Question: What are you demanding that God knows isn't best?

DAY 168

"Give therefore thy servant an understanding heart to judge thy people." — 1 Kings 3:9 (KJV)

Solomon could have asked for anything. He asked for wisdom. God threw in wealth and honor as a bonus. When you ask for the right things, God adds the rest things. Your prayer requests reveal your priorities. Solomon's request revealed a heart that valued wisdom over wealth. God provides abundantly when our asks align with His heart.

Reflection Question: What should you be asking for instead of what you've been requesting?

DAY 169

"And the man of God said, Where fell it? And he shewed him the place." —
2 Kings 6:6 (KJV)

A borrowed axe head sank. Career crisis for a poor prophet student. Elisha made iron swim. God cares about your work tools, your borrowed things, your practical problems. That practical need you think is too small for God—He made iron float. Your lost tool, broken equipment, work crisis—God does practical miracles for working people.

Reflection Question: What practical problem needs a miraculous solution?

DAY 170

"Behold, I have commanded a widow woman there to sustain thee." — *1 Kings 17:9 (KJV)*

God commanded a broke widow to feed a prophet. She didn't know she was commanded—she was planning to die. Your provision might come through someone who doesn't look like a provider. The least likely source might be God's chosen channel. That person you think has nothing to offer might be commanded to sustain you. Don't judge the vessel; just receive the provision.

Reflection Question: What unlikely source might God be commanding to provide for you?

DAY 171

"But the Lord was with Joseph, and shewed him mercy, and gave him favour." — Genesis 39:21 (KJV)

Joseph prospered in prison. Not after prison—in prison. Your worst place might become your blessed place. Provision isn't always about location change; sometimes it's about favor despite location. Prison became Joseph's preparation ground. What looked like punishment was actually positioning. Your restrictive situation might be God's provision in disguise.

Reflection Question: How might your prison actually be provision?

DAY 172

"And when they had brought their ships to land, they forsook all, and followed him." — Luke 5:11 (KJV)

Greatest catch of their career, then they left it all. Sometimes God provides abundance to show you it's not your source—He is. The miraculous catch was proof, not provision. They could have stayed and built a fishing empire. Instead, the provision became permission to leave. Your breakthrough might be God showing you what you don't need to chase.

Reflection Question: What provision might God be using to free you, not tie you down?

DAY 173

"And the barrel of meal wasted not, neither did the cruse of oil fail, according to the word of the Lord." — *1 Kings 17:16 (KJV)*

She started with a handful and fed three people for years. God didn't fill the barrel—He just made sure it never emptied. Sometimes provision is stretching what you have, not getting what you don't. That little you're managing—what if God wants to stretch it rather than replace it? The widow's handful became history because she shared it instead of saved it.

Reflection Question: What handful needs to be shared for it to be stretched?

DAY 174

"And he called the name of that place Bethel: for there he said, God hath met me." — *Genesis 28:19 (KJV)*

Jacob slept on a rock and saw heaven open. His worst night became his worship site. That place of lack might be where heaven opens. Your Beth-el might be disguised as your bad situation. He set up a memorial where he met God, not where life was comfortable. Your hardest place might become your holiest place. God shows up in lack to prove He's enough.

Reflection Question: What difficult place might be your Beth-el in disguise?

DAY 175

"And Isaac digged again the wells of water, which they had digged in the days of Abraham." — *Genesis 26:18 (KJV)*

Isaac didn't dig new wells—he recovered old ones. Sometimes provision is restoration, not innovation. That old resource, relationship, or skill you abandoned might need re-digging. The Philistines had filled Abraham's wells with dirt. Your past provision might be buried under disappointment. Isaac's water was already there—it just needed excavation.

Reflection Question: What old well needs re-digging in your life?

DAY 176

"And after a time he returned...and he turned aside to see the carcase of the lion: and, behold, there was a swarm of bees and honey." — *Judges 14:8 (KJV)*

Samson found honey where a lion died. Sweetness in the place of past attack. Your old battle ground might become your provision ground. Where the enemy tried to kill you might be where God feeds you. He ate the honey and shared it. Your worst experience might become your best provision—not just for you but for others. Sometimes you have to revisit where you were attacked to find the honey.

Reflection Question: What past attack might now hold provision?

DAY 177

"And he took the blind man by the hand...and when he had spit on his eyes, and put his hands upon him, he asked him if he saw ought." — Mark 8:23 (KJV)

First touch: partial sight. Second touch: clear vision. Sometimes provision comes in stages. That partial answer, incomplete healing, almost-breakthrough—maybe you need a second touch. Jesus could have healed completely the first time. The progressive miracle teaches us that partial provision might be intentional, not insufficient. Don't settle, but don't despise the process.

Reflection Question: Where do you need to ask for the second touch?

DAY 178

"And the dove came in to him in the evening; and, lo, in her mouth was an olive leaf." — Genesis 8:11 (KJV)

After the flood, a dove brought evidence of dry land. Your provision evidence might come through something small and easily missed. That tiny sign might be announcing major change. Noah didn't see the land—he saw a leaf. Sometimes God sends tokens before totality. That small sign of provision might be the preview of coming restoration.

Reflection Question: What small sign might be previewing bigger provision?

DAY 179

"Yea, forty years didst thou sustain them in the wilderness, so that they lacked nothing; their clothes waxed not old." — Nehemiah 9:21 (KJV)

Forty years, same outfit, perfect fit. Kids grew, clothes grew. That's weird provision—not new clothes but supernatural stretching. God can make what you have fit what you need. Your resources might not need replacing—they might need supernatural stretching. What seems insufficient might be supernaturally elastic. God can make your current fit your future.

Reflection Question: What current resource needs supernatural stretching?

DAY 180

"And Simon answering said unto him, Master, we have toiled all the night, and have taken nothing: nevertheless at thy word I will let down the net." — Luke 5:5 (KJV)

All night, empty nets. One word from Jesus, nets breaking. Your empty might be one word away from overflow. The difference between nothing and abundance was obedience to "nevertheless." Peter argued first—they'd tried all night in prime fishing time. Sometimes provision requires doing the same thing differently—with Jesus' instruction. Your empty nets might just need His word.

Reflection Question: What "nevertheless" instruction do you need to obey?

DAY 181

"And Jesus took the loaves; and when he had given thanks, he distributed to the disciples." — John 6:11 (KJV)

Five thousand men, plus women and children—probably fifteen thousand people. Five loaves. That's God's math: insufficient + gratitude = abundance. Jesus gave thanks for not enough, then distributed more than enough. The multiplication happened in distribution, not storage. As they gave it away, it grew. Your provision might multiply in giving, not keeping. Heaven's economics: the more you distribute, the more you have.

Reflection Question: What needs to be distributed to be multiplied?

July: Wisdom and Understanding

Day 182

"Give therefore thy servant an understanding heart to judge thy people, that I may discern between good and bad." — 1 Kings 3:9 (KJV)

Solomon could've asked for anything—unlimited wealth, crushing his enemies, a longer life. God basically handed him a blank check. What does the young king request? Wisdom. That's like winning the lottery and asking for good judgment about money instead of the money itself. But here's what happened: God was so impressed, He threw in everything else as a bonus. Solomon got the wealth, the respect, the whole package—because he asked for the one thing that would help him handle it all. It's like asking for fishing lessons instead of fish. One feeds you today; the other feeds you forever. Your prayer requests say a lot about what you value. Solomon knew that without wisdom, even blessings become burdens.

Reflection Question: If God gave you one request, would you ask for the prize or the wisdom to handle it?

DAY 183

"The fool hath said in his heart, There is no God." — Psalm 14:1 (KJV)

Notice it says "in his heart," not "with his mind." This isn't about intelligence—plenty of smart people are fools, and simple people can be wise. The fool's problem is excluding God from the equation. You see it everywhere: the businessman who built an empire but lost his family, the athlete who gained fame but lost himself. They're not stupid—they just ignored the Referee. That decision you're overanalyzing? You've consulted everyone except the One who knows the outcome. Foolishness isn't being wrong about facts; it's being wrong about what truly matters.

Reflection Question: Where have you been making "smart" decisions while forgetting to include God?

DAY 184

"I wisdom dwell with prudence, and find out knowledge of witty inventions." — Proverbs 8:12 (KJV)

Wisdom isn't some mystical knowledge—it's practical, living with prudence and hanging out with discretion. Think of it as street smarts for the soul, knowing which battles to fight and when to walk away. It's reading the room spiritually. That uneasy feeling you can't explain? Wisdom's tapping your shoulder. That strange peace while others panic? Wisdom again. She's often a quiet voice saying "wait" when everything else screams "now." God's wisdom brings creative solutions—like using a slingshot against full armor.

Reflection Question: What situation needs God's creative wisdom instead of conventional solutions?

DAY 185

"Go to the ant, thou sluggard; consider her ways, and be wise." — Proverbs 6:6 (KJV)

God tells us to take leadership lessons from an ant. Without a boss or perfect conditions, she works on winter's problems during summer—no procrastination, no excuses. While we hit snooze, waiting for inspiration, the ant shows that wisdom often looks like boring consistency. She's not trying to go viral—just steadily carrying crumbs heavier than herself. Your breakthrough might not need a miracle but ant-like wisdom: small, consistent actions, preparing today for tomorrow's demands. The ant never gave a TED talk, but Solomon said to learn from her.

Reflection Question: What "ant work" have you been avoiding while waiting for something more spectacular?

DAY 186

"If thou seekest her as silver, and searchest for her as for hid treasures." — Proverbs 2:4 (KJV)

Nobody stumbles upon buried treasure—it takes maps, shovels, and effort. Solomon says wisdom requires the same intensity. You won't find it while mindlessly scrolling your phone; it demands the focus of a treasure hunter. Think about how you search for lost car keys—flipping cushions, retracing steps, checking pockets repeatedly. That desperation is how we should pursue wisdom. Yet most of us work harder at finding a good parking spot than seeking wisdom. Like treasure, wisdom is valuable, hidden, and worth every ounce of effort to uncover.

Reflection Question: Are you pursuing wisdom with treasure-hunter intensity or hoping it randomly appears?

DAY 187

"Miserable comforters are ye all." — *Job 16:2 (KJV)*

Job's friends had all the answers—quoting scripture, making logical arguments, sounding spiritual—and they were completely wrong. They couldn't handle mystery, insisting Job's suffering must be his fault. Bad theology with good intentions still hurts people. Life isn't that clean—sometimes bad things happen to good people, and wisdom accepts the mystery. Your friend going through hell doesn't need theories or lectures. Sometimes wisdom means showing up with pizza and staying quiet. Job's friends would have done more good by saying less and simply being present.

Reflection Question: Where do you need to offer presence instead of answers?

DAY 188

"The fear of the Lord is the beginning of wisdom." — *Proverbs 9:10 (KJV)*

Fear of God isn't cowering terror—it's awe mixed with respect, like standing at the edge of the Grand Canyon. You're amazed but also mindful of the drop, and that respect keeps you from reckless behavior. It's the beginning of wisdom, not the end—like learning to drive begins with respecting a car's power. You don't stay terrified, but you never forget the responsibility. True wisdom starts with knowing who God is and who you're not. Without the fear of God, wisdom becomes mere human cleverness—impressive but ultimately limited.

Reflection Question: Have you become too casual with God, losing the awe that produces wisdom?

DAY 189

"Wisdom crieth without; she uttereth her voice in the streets." — Proverbs 1:20 (KJV)

Wisdom isn't hiding in a monastery or locked behind seminary doors—she's in the streets, shouting at the intersection, trying to get your attention. The problem isn't her silence; it's our lack of listening. She's competing with countless voices—pings, news, opinions—but wisdom often says the opposite of what's trending. She says "slow down" when culture screams "hustle harder," or "forgive" when you want revenge. The street reference matters—wisdom is practical, accessible, and present in everyday life, not just in Sunday services. She's there, ready, if you're willing to listen.

Reflection Question: What is wisdom trying to tell you that you keep drowning out with noise?

DAY 190

"And all Israel heard of the judgment which the king had judged; and they feared the king: for they saw that the wisdom of God was in him." — 1 Kings 3:28 (KJV)

Solomon's first judgment—two women, one baby, both claiming to be the mother—was solved by threatening to cut the baby in half. It sounded insane but instantly revealed the true mother. That's wisdom: seeing past the surface to the heart. Solomon was young, inexperienced, and following a legendary father, but wisdom isn't about age. The oldest person in the room isn't always the wisest. Wisdom comes from God, not years. Feeling too young or inexperienced? God's wisdom has no age requirement—it's available to anyone connected to Him.

Reflection Question: Where has your age become an excuse for not operating in wisdom?

DAY 191

"A wise son heareth his father's instruction: but a scorner heareth not rebuke." — Proverbs 13:1 (KJV)

The scorner always has a comeback, treating wisdom like a joke and correction as an insult, with a smirk that says, "I know better." Over time, his confidence becomes his cage—he can't grow because he won't listen, and his mockery of wisdom turns into a prophecy of his own foolishness. Meanwhile, the wise person, though correction stings, embraces it and grows stronger. The difference isn't intelligence; it's teachability. The scorner might win the argument, but he loses the lesson.

Reflection Question: Where has your need to be right prevented you from getting wise?

DAY 192

"Then this Daniel was preferred above the presidents and princes, because an excellent spirit was in him." — Daniel 6:3 (KJV)

Daniel didn't just survive Babylon—he thrived. Four kings, multiple regime changes, and yet he kept getting promoted. His secret? An excellent spirit—not just skill or knowledge, but spiritual excellence that made him irreplaceable. Daniel made heathen kings look good, with wisdom that worked even in hostile environments. While others played politics, Daniel followed heaven's rules and still won earth's games. That's what true wisdom does—it works anywhere, under any conditions. Your workplace might feel like Babylon, but Daniel proves you can have wisdom and excellence that transcend the system, beyond what résumés can explain.

Reflection Question: How could spiritual excellence make you irreplaceable in secular spaces?

DAY 193

"The testimony of the Lord is sure, making wise the simple." — *Psalm 19:7 (KJV)*

God's Word doesn't just inform smart people—it makes simple people wise. You don't need a degree to understand what God's saying. His testimony is sure, reliable, consistent. It turns regular folks into wise ones. That intimidation you feel about not knowing enough? God specializes in making the simple wise. His Word is the great equalizer. The CEO and the janitor have access to the same wisdom. The PhD and the GED can both become wise through scripture. The Bible isn't just for scholars—it's for anyone who wants wisdom bad enough to read it.

Reflection Question: Have you been disqualifying yourself from wisdom because you feel too simple?

DAY 194

"For wisdom is better than rubies; and all the things that may be desired are not to be compared to it." — *Proverbs 8:11 (KJV)*

Rubies you can lose. Stock markets crash. Houses burn. But wisdom? Once you have it, it's yours forever. It compounds daily, works in any economy, transfers to every situation. You can't inherit money without losing value to taxes, but you can inherit wisdom tax-free. We spend fortunes on education but won't spend time seeking wisdom. We'll drive across town to save five dollars on gas but won't walk across the room to pick up the Bible. We know the price of everything but the value of wisdom. Solomon had both—unlimited wealth and wisdom. Guess which one he said was better?

Reflection Question: What are you chasing that's worth less than wisdom?

DAY 195

"Wisdom is a defence, and money is a defence: but the excellency of knowledge is, that wisdom giveth life to them that have it." — Ecclesiastes 7:12 (KJV)

Money can protect you from some things—it buys better lawyers, healthcare, and security systems. But wisdom preserves life itself. It keeps you from needing the lawyer or the security system in the first place. Wisdom warns you which relationships to avoid, which investments to skip, and which words to hold back. It's preventative medicine for the soul. Money might bail you out; wisdom keeps you from needing bail. One is a band-aid; the other is prevention. The rich young ruler had money but lacked the wisdom to follow Jesus. Which defense would you rather have?

Reflection Question: Where have you been relying on money to solve what wisdom could prevent?

DAY 196

"Give me now wisdom and knowledge, that I may go out and come in before this people." — 2 Chronicles 1:10 (KJV)

"Go out and come in"—that's daily life, the regular routines, the everyday decisions. Solomon didn't ask for wisdom just for the big moments; he needed it for the mundane Tuesday afternoon choices that quietly shape a life. Wisdom isn't just for crisis management—it's for knowing when to speak up in a meeting or stay silent, how to handle a difficult customer, raise teenagers, or manage money. The ordinary stuff that doesn't feel spiritual but changes everything. You need wisdom for your commute as much as your calling.

Reflection Question: What daily routine needs wisdom applied to it?

DAY 197

"Her ways are ways of pleasantness, and all her paths are peace." —
Proverbs 3:17 (KJV)

Wisdom doesn't lead to misery—her paths are pleasant and peaceful. If following God feels like constant stress and strife, you might be following rules, not wisdom. Wisdom knows how to rest, laugh, and live without losing your mind. That doesn't mean it's easy—pleasant and easy aren't the same—but there's peace in doing things God's way, even when it's hard. Like the satisfaction of paying cash instead of credit or the peace of a clear conscience. Wisdom's path might be uphill, but the view is worth it. Religion complicates; wisdom simplifies. One binds, the other frees.

Reflection Question: Is your spiritual path peaceful, or have you complicated wisdom with religion?

DAY 198

"He giveth wisdom unto the wise, and knowledge to them that know understanding." — Daniel 2:21 (KJV)

It seems backwards—giving wisdom to the wise—but wisdom attracts more wisdom, like compound interest for your soul. The more you use it, the more you get, as every wise decision positions you for greater understanding. Daniel understood this; he didn't rely on yesterday's wisdom but kept seeking, learning, and growing, which is why he could interpret dreams that mystified others. Meanwhile, fools lose even the little understanding they have because wisdom is a use-it-or-lose-it currency.

Reflection Question: How can you invest the wisdom you have to gain more?

DAY 199

"The mouth of the righteous speaketh wisdom, and his tongue talketh of judgment." — Psalm 37:30 (KJV)

Your mouth reveals your wisdom level faster than your résumé. Within five minutes of conversation, people know if you're wise or just smart. Wisdom doesn't need to announce itself—it's obvious when someone speaks. The righteous don't speak to impress but to bless. Their words build rather than burn. They know when to talk and when to listen, what to say and what to skip. That's wisdom—not just having the right answer but knowing when to share it. Your tongue is preaching a sermon about your wisdom every time you open your mouth.

Reflection Question: What does your speech pattern reveal about your wisdom level?

DAY 200

"Length of days is in her right hand; and in her left hand riches and honour." — Proverbs 3:16 (KJV)

Wisdom comes with benefits—long life in one hand, riches and honor in the other. Not because wisdom is a magic formula, but because wise living naturally produces good outcomes. You make better decisions, avoid costly mistakes, build stronger relationships. The fool might get rich quick, but wisdom gets rich right. The fool might live fast, but wisdom lives long. It's not prosperity gospel—it's practical reality. Wise choices compound into blessed lives. Foolish choices compound into complicated ones. Both hands are full. Wisdom doesn't make you choose between length of life and quality of life.

Reflection Question: Which hand of wisdom's reward do you need to receive?

DAY 201

"But the wisdom that is from above is first pure, then peaceable, gentle, and easy to be intreated." — James 3:17 (KJV)

Heaven's wisdom has a signature. It's pure—no hidden agendas. Peaceable—not starting fights for fun. Gentle—strong but not harsh. Easy to be entreated—approachable, not arrogant. If your "wisdom" is causing chaos, it might not be from above. You can tell wisdom's source by its fruit. Earthly wisdom divides, competes, manipulates. Heavenly wisdom unites, serves, builds. One creates drama; the other creates peace. Check your wisdom's fruit—it'll tell you which tree it came from. Some people have knowledge that destroys. God's wisdom always builds.

Reflection Question: Is your wisdom creating peace or problems?

DAY 202

"If any of you lack wisdom, let him ask of God, that giveth to all men liberally, and upbraideth not." — James 1:5 (KJV)

God's not stingy with wisdom. He gives it liberally—generously, abundantly, without making you feel stupid for asking. You don't have to earn it, deserve it, or prove you'll use it right. Just ask. That problem you've been trying to figure out on your own? God's got wisdom for it, and He's not holding back. He won't lecture you about why you should already know. He won't make you feel dumb for needing help. He just gives wisdom liberally to whoever asks. The only thing keeping you from wisdom is not asking for it.

Reflection Question: What situation needs you to simply ask God for wisdom?

DAY 203

"And the spirit of the Lord shall rest upon him, the spirit of wisdom and understanding." — Isaiah 11:2 (KJV)

Wisdom and understanding are twins—you need both. Wisdom knows what; understanding knows why. Wisdom sees the rule; understanding grasps the reason. Together, they give you the full picture. Jesus had both. He knew the law (wisdom) and the heart behind it (understanding). That's why He could honor Sabbath while healing on it. He understood the why behind the what. Religious leaders had wisdom without understanding—they kept rules but missed relationship. You might know what the Bible says but miss what God means.

Reflection Question: Where do you have wisdom but lack understanding?

DAY 204

"With him is wisdom and strength, he hath counsel and understanding." — Job 12:13 (KJV)

God doesn't just have good ideas—He has the power to execute them. His wisdom comes with strength. His counsel includes capability. That's the difference between human advice and divine wisdom: God can actually do what He says. Your adviser might have great strategies but no ability to help implement them. God's wisdom includes the strength to accomplish it. When He gives you counsel, He also provides the might to carry it out. The plan and the power come in the same package. Stop separating wisdom from strength—God provides both.

Reflection Question: What counsel from God are you treating as suggestion instead of empowerment?

DAY 205

"But thou, O Daniel, shut up the words, and seal the book, even to the time of the end: many shall run to and fro, and knowledge shall be increased."
— Daniel 12:4 (KJV)

We're living this prophecy. Knowledge doubles every twelve hours now. We have more information in our pocket than entire civilizations possessed. But are we wiser? Information without wisdom is just noise. You can Google anything in seconds, but Google can't tell you what to do with what you know. Knowledge tells you how to build a bomb; wisdom tells you why you shouldn't. We're drowning in knowledge but thirsting for wisdom. The increase of knowledge makes wisdom more valuable, not less.

Reflection Question: Where has information overload replaced wisdom in your life?

DAY 206

"For the wisdom of this world is foolishness with God." — 1 Corinthians 3:19 (KJV)

The world's wisdom says look out for number one, climb the ladder, win at any cost. God calls that foolishness. What gets applause on earth might get eye-rolls in heaven. The wisdom that builds empires might destroy souls. This world's wisdom has an expiration date. It works until it doesn't. It impresses until eternity. It profits until judgment. That's why millionaires jump from buildings and successful people feel empty. They followed wisdom that leads nowhere eternal. God's foolishness outsmarts earth's wisdom every time.

Reflection Question: What worldly wisdom do you need to exchange for godly foolishness?

DAY 207

"And wisdom and knowledge shall be the stability of thy times, and strength of salvation." — Isaiah 33:6 (KJV)

In unstable times, wisdom stabilizes. When everything's shaking, wisdom is the foundation that doesn't move. Markets crash, governments fail, relationships end—but wisdom remains stable currency in any economy. That's why Daniel thrived through four different administrations. His wisdom worked regardless of who sat on the throne. Your stability doesn't come from circumstances but from wisdom that transcends circumstances. In shaking seasons, wisdom is your anchor.

Reflection Question: How can wisdom stabilize your current instability?

DAY 208

"Wisdom is the principal thing; therefore get wisdom: and with all thy getting get understanding." — Proverbs 4:7 (KJV)

Principal means first, chief, most important. Everything else is secondary. You're getting degrees, promotions, possessions—but are you getting wisdom? You can get everything else and miss the principal thing. It's like focusing on car accessories while ignoring the engine. Sure, those rims look nice, but if the engine doesn't work, you've got an expensive paperweight. Wisdom is the engine that makes everything else work. With all your getting—your hustling, achieving, accumulating—get wisdom.

Reflection Question: What have you been getting instead of the principal thing?

DAY 209

"Take fast hold of instruction; let her not go: keep her; for she is thy life."
— Proverbs 4:13 (KJV)

Grip instruction like your life depends on it—because it does. Not casually, not loosely, but fast hold. Like hanging from a cliff. That's how tightly we should hold wisdom. But we hold our phones tighter than we hold instruction. "She is thy life"—not part of your life, not addition to your life, but life itself. Every instruction you release, you lose life. Every wisdom you ignore costs you something. The instruction you're treating as optional might be essential. Stop letting go of what you should be gripping.

Reflection Question: What instruction have you been holding loosely that needs a tighter grip?

DAY 210

"According to the grace of God which is given unto me, as a wise masterbuilder, I have laid the foundation." — 1 Corinthians 3:10 (KJV)

Paul didn't call himself a passionate builder or a sincere builder—he said wise builder. Passion without wisdom builds crooked. Sincerity without wisdom builds weak. You need wisdom to build anything that lasts. Every man is building something—a family, career, reputation, legacy. But are you building wisely? The storms will reveal whether you built with wisdom or just enthusiasm. Good intentions don't replace good foundations. Wise builders think about storms during sunshine.

Reflection Question: What are you building with zeal but without wisdom?

DAY 211

"But we speak the wisdom of God in a mystery, even the hidden wisdom, which God ordained before the world." — 1 Corinthians 2:7 (KJV)

Some wisdom is hidden, requiring revelation to see it. It's not secret to be exclusive but hidden to be discovered. Like Easter eggs for the soul—God hides wisdom for you, not from you. This wisdom was ordained before the world began. Before your problem existed, God had wisdom for it. Before your question formed, the answer was prepared. The wisdom you need isn't being created—it's waiting to be revealed. What looks mysterious has divine wisdom hidden in it.

Reflection Question: What mystery in your life might be hiding wisdom?

DAY 212

"Wisdom hath builded her house, she hath hewn out her seven pillars." — Proverbs 9:1 (KJV)

Wisdom doesn't rent; she builds. Not a shack but a house with seven pillars—complete, stable, permanent. She's not camping out in your life; she wants to construct something lasting. But building takes time, and we want microwave wisdom. Seven pillars means she's thorough. No cutting corners, no rush jobs. Each pillar carefully hewn, properly placed. Your life might be under construction because wisdom is building something worth living in. Let wisdom finish what she's building.

Reflection Question: Which pillar of wisdom is currently under construction in your life?

AUGUST: PERSEVERANCE AND ENDURANCE

DAY 213

"And let us not be weary in well doing: for in due season we shall reap, if we faint not." — *Galatians 6:9 (KJV)*

"Due season"—not your season, not when you want it, but when it's due. Like fruit that won't ripen faster just because you're hungry. Paul says don't get weary, don't faint. Easier said than done when you've been sowing for years with no harvest in sight. That ministry that feels pointless, that marriage you keep investing in, that teenager you keep praying for—the harvest is coming. But fainting forfeits the crop. You might be three days from breakthrough and not know it. The farmer doesn't dig up seeds to check progress. Neither should you. Due season always arrives for those who don't faint.

Reflection Question: What field are you tempted to abandon right before harvest?

DAY 214

"My brethren, count it all joy when ye fall into divers temptations; Knowing this, that the trying of your faith worketh patience." — *James 1:2-3 (KJV)*

"Count it all joy"? James must be joking. Your business is failing, your health declining, your kids rebelling—and you're supposed to celebrate? But James knows pressure creates diamonds, not just crushed coal. The difference is time and endurance. Trials aren't trying to break you; they're building you. Like muscles, patience grows under resistance. You don't get stronger lifting empty bars. The weight that feels crushing is actually constructing—if you endure it long enough. Your trial isn't punishment; it's your trainer.

Reflection Question: What pressure are you under that might be creating a diamond?

DAY 215

"Wherefore seeing we also are compassed about with so great a cloud of witnesses...let us run with patience the race that is set before us." — *Hebrews 12:1 (KJV)*

This isn't a sprint; it's a marathon. You can't run a marathon like a hundred-meter dash—you'll collapse by mile two. The race set before you requires patience, pacing, persistence. Everyone looks fast for the first mile. That cloud of witnesses? They're not spectators; they're finishers. Abraham, Moses, David—they all wanted to quit at mile thirteen. But they kept running. Now they're cheering for you, saying, "Keep going! We made it; so can you!" Pace yourself. This race is longer than you think.

Reflection Question: Where are you sprinting in a marathon season?

DAY 216

"Ye have heard of the patience of Job, and have seen the end of the Lord; that the Lord is very pitiful, and of tender mercy." — James 5:11 (KJV)

Everyone knows Job suffered. Not everyone remembers he got double back. We focus on the loss and forget the restoration. James says look at "the end of the Lord"—how God finished Job's story. The ending changes everything about the middle. Job didn't know he was in chapter 3 of a 42-chapter book. He thought his story was over when it was just turning. Your current chapter might be brutal, but it's not your conclusion. God's not done writing. Job's patience wasn't perfect, but it was persistent.

Reflection Question: What if your worst chapter isn't your last chapter?

DAY 217

"And not only so, but we glory in tribulations also: knowing that tribulation worketh patience." — Romans 5:3 (KJV)

Tribulation is your trainer. Nobody likes the gym at 5 AM, but everyone likes the results. Paul says glory in tribulations— not because pain feels good, but because you know what it's producing. That resistance you're pushing against is building spiritual muscle. You want patience without tribulation. That's like wanting muscles without workouts. Doesn't happen. Every trial is a rep, every problem is resistance training. The weight that feels unbearable is building strength you'll need later. Tribulation is the gym where patience gets built.

Reflection Question: What tribulation is currently working patience in you?

DAY 218

"And thou shalt remember all the way which the Lord thy God led thee these forty years in the wilderness." — Deuteronomy 8:2 (KJV)

Forty years for an eleven-day journey. That's not poor navigation; that's purposeful preparation. The wilderness wasn't punishment—it was prep school for the Promised Land. Every extra year was adding something they'd need. Your extended wilderness might be extended education. That promotion that's taking forever, that breakthrough that keeps getting delayed—maybe you're not ready for where you're going. The wilderness is building muscles the Promised Land will require. Some destinations require forty years of preparation for eleven days of journey.

Reflection Question: What is your extended wilderness teaching you?

DAY 219

"Wherefore take unto you the whole armour of God, that ye may be able to withstand in the evil day, and having done all, to stand." — Ephesians 6:13 (KJV)

After you've done everything—prayed, fasted, believed, confessed—then what? Stand. Just stand. Sometimes the most spiritual thing is the most stubborn thing: refusing to move. Not advancing, not retreating, just standing. Standing doesn't feel heroic. It feels like nothing's happening. But sometimes the battle is won by whoever remains standing when the dust settles. You've done all you can do. Now do the hardest thing: stand still and see salvation. Sometimes victory is simply outlasting the attack.

Reflection Question: Where do you need to stop doing and start standing?

DAY 220

"For consider him that endured such contradiction of sinners against himself, lest ye be wearied and faint in your minds." — Hebrews 12:3 (KJV)

When you want to quit, consider Jesus. He endured more contradiction than you ever will. Perfect God, called demon-possessed. Sinless Savior, crucified with criminals. He endured the ultimate injustice without giving up. Your contradiction feels unbearable—being misunderstood, falsely accused, unfairly treated. But consider Him. He endured worse and won. Your mind wants to quit before your body does. That's where the battle is—between your ears. Consider Him, and keep going.

Reflection Question: How does considering Christ's endurance change your perspective on yours?

DAY 221

"Rest in the Lord, and wait patiently for him: fret not thyself because of him who prospereth in his way." — Psalm 37:7 (KJV)

Waiting patiently while watching the wicked prosper—that's graduate-level faith. Your dishonest competitor gets the contract. Your manipulative coworker gets promoted. Meanwhile, you're doing right and going nowhere. David says rest, wait, don't fret. Their prosperity has an expiration date; your patience doesn't. What looks like them winning is just a middle chapter, not the final score. God's timing is perfect, even when it feels perfectly wrong. Rest isn't passive—it's trusting God's timeline over your timetable.

Reflection Question: Whose prosperity is making you impatient with God's timing?

DAY 222

"While the earth remaineth, seedtime and harvest, cold and heat, and summer and winter, and day and night shall not cease." — Genesis 8:22 (KJV)

After the flood, God promised rhythms would remain. Seedtime always comes before harvest. You can't skip seedtime because you're hungry. That season of sowing when nothing's showing—it's not broken; it's biblical. You want to live in perpetual harvest, but God designed seasons. Your winter isn't failure; it's a season. Your seedtime isn't wasted; it's invested. The rhythm that frustrates you is the rhythm that sustains everything. Trust the rhythm even when you can't see results.

Reflection Question: Are you trying to harvest in your seedtime season?

DAY 223

"That ye be not slothful, but followers of them who through faith and patience inherit the promises." — Hebrews 6:12 (KJV)

Faith and patience—you need both. Faith believes the promise; patience waits for it. Faith sees it; patience stands until it shows up. Most of us have faith or patience, but promises require both. Abraham had faith for a son but needed patience for twenty-five years. Faith got him started; patience got him through. Your promise might not be missing; it might be marinating. Some promises take decades to develop. Faith without patience quits too soon.

Reflection Question: Which do you need more of right now—faith or patience?

DAY 224

"By faith he forsook Egypt, not fearing the wrath of the king: for he endured, as seeing him who is invisible." — Hebrews 11:27 (KJV)

Moses endured by seeing the invisible. That's the secret—looking at what you can't see rather than what you can. The invisible God was more real to Moses than the visible Pharaoh. That's how you endure the unbearable. Your visible circumstances are screaming, but what's invisible is whispering. Which voice are you following? Moses could endure Egypt because he saw beyond Egypt. Your endurance is proportional to your eternal perspective. See the invisible, endure the impossible.

Reflection Question: What invisible reality do you need to focus on more than visible circumstances?

DAY 225

"Weeping may endure for a night, but joy cometh in the morning." — Psalm 30:5 (KJV)

Night feels eternal when you're in it. Three AM thoughts hit different. The darkness whispers that dawn isn't coming. But David says weeping has an expiration time—night. Joy has an appointment—morning. Your night might be a season, not sixty minutes. But morning is programmed into creation. It always comes. That grief, that loss, that pain—it's not permanent; it's nocturnal. Joy isn't hoping; it's coming. The longest night eventually surrenders to dawn.

Reflection Question: What night season are you in that morning is coming to?

DAY 226

"And now, behold, the Lord hath kept me alive, as he said, these forty and five years...and now, lo, I am this day fourscore and five years old." —
Joshua 14:10 (KJV)

Caleb waited forty-five years for his promise. Not forty-five days or months—years. At eighty-five, he finally got his mountain. Most people retire; Caleb was just getting started. His patience outlasted everyone else's doubt. That promise God gave you decades ago? Caleb says keep believing. Age doesn't cancel promises. Time doesn't nullify God's word. Caleb's strength at eighty-five matched his faith at forty. Some promises are worth a forty-five-year wait.

Reflection Question: What old promise do you need to keep believing for?

DAY 227

"And daily in the temple, and in every house, they ceased not to teach and preach Jesus Christ." — Acts 5:42 (KJV)

They were beaten, threatened, imprisoned. Their response? They "ceased not." That's persistence—preaching through pain, teaching through threats. The opposition that should have stopped them only spread them. "Ceased not"—what a phrase. No breaks, no backing down, no burnout. How? Because persecution confirmed they were doing something right. If hell wasn't worried, it wouldn't fight so hard. Your opposition might be confirmation, not contradiction.

Reflection Question: What are you ceasing that you should continue despite opposition?

DAY 228

"They which builded on the wall, and they that bare burdens, with those that laded, every one with one of his hands wrought in the work, and with the other hand held a weapon." — Nehemiah 4:17 (KJV)

Trowel in one hand, sword in the other. Building and battling simultaneously. That's your life—trying to construct while defending against destruction. Nehemiah's builders teach us that sometimes you can't wait for perfect conditions. You're building a marriage while fighting financial pressure. Raising kids while battling your own issues. Growing faith while fighting doubt. One hand builds; one hand battles. That's not dysfunction; that's normal. Progress happens while problems persist.

Reflection Question: What are you building with one hand while battling with the other?

DAY 229

"I will stand upon my watch, and set me upon the tower, and will watch to see what he will say unto me." — Habakkuk 2:1 (KJV)

Habakkuk took his position and waited. Not casually but intentionally—on his watch, upon his tower. He positioned himself to hear from God, then waited. That's different from passive waiting. It's active positioning. Your answer might be waiting for you to take position. That quiet time you skip, that prayer place you avoid—what if answers are waiting there? Habakkuk didn't wait wherever; he waited strategically. Position yourself, then wait patiently.

Reflection Question: What position do you need to take while waiting for God's answer?

DAY 230

"Thou therefore endure hardness, as a good soldier of Jesus Christ." — 2 Timothy 2:3 (KJV)

Soldiers expect hardness. They don't complain about early mornings, uncomfortable conditions, or difficult missions. It comes with the uniform. Paul says endure hardness like a soldier—expecting it, not exemption from it. You signed up for war, not vacation. That spiritual battle, that difficult assignment, that uncomfortable calling—you're not being punished; you're being deployed. Good soldiers don't desert when deployment gets difficult. Hardness isn't hazing; it's part of the job.

Reflection Question: What hardness do you need to endure as a good soldier?

DAY 231

"My flesh and my heart faileth: but God is the strength of my heart, and my portion for ever." — Psalm 73:26 (KJV)

Your flesh will fail—that's not pessimism; it's promise. Your strength has limits. Your heart will falter. But right when flesh fails, God's strength shows up. He's not your backup plan; He's your strength when you have none left. That moment when you can't take another step, make another call, face another day—that's when God carries you. Not helps you walk, but carries you. Your failure becomes His opportunity to be your strength. Flesh failing isn't the end; it's the exchange.

Reflection Question: Where is your flesh failing and God's strength available?

DAY 232

"But let patience have her perfect work, that ye may be perfect and entire, wanting nothing." — James 1:4 (KJV)

Patience isn't just waiting; she's working. While you're frustrated about delays, patience is perfecting something in you. She's not wasting time; she's working overtime to make you complete. That delay you hate might be patience doing detail work. Quick fixes leave cracks; patience creates completeness. You want the shortcut, but shortcuts short-circuit the perfect work patience is performing. Let patience finish what she started.

Reflection Question: What perfect work is patience trying to complete in you?

DAY 233

"Hope deferred maketh the heart sick: but when the desire cometh, it is a tree of life." — Proverbs 13:12 (KJV)

That sick feeling when promises delay? Solomon says it's real—hope deferred makes hearts sick. You're not weak for feeling discouraged when waiting extends. But notice the second part: when it comes, it's a tree of life. Trees don't appear overnight. They grow slowly, secretly, steadily. Your deferred hope is growing roots you can't see. When it finally breaks through, it won't be a flower that fades but a tree that lasts. Heart sickness is sometimes labor pains for trees of life.

Reflection Question: What deferred hope might be growing into a tree of life?

DAY 234

"Wherefore seeing we also are compassed about with so great a cloud of witnesses." — Hebrews 12:1 (KJV)

You're not running alone. Moses is watching. David is cheering. Paul is in the stands. Every saint who finished is witnessing your race. They're not judging your pace; they're encouraging your persistence. They faced what you're facing and finished. Their testimony is your evidence that finishing is possible. When you want to quit, remember: Abraham wanted to quit too. But he didn't, and neither should you. The cloud isn't watching you fail; they're watching you finish.

Reflection Question: Whose testimony in the cloud of witnesses encourages you most?

DAY 235

"And let us not be weary in well doing: for in due season we shall reap, if we faint not." — Galatians 6:9 (KJV)

"If we faint not"—that's the condition. Fainting forfeits the harvest. Not failing, not falling, but fainting—giving up right before breakthrough. The enemy knows he can't stop your harvest, so he tries to make you faint before it arrives. That weariness in well-doing? It hits hardest right before harvest. Farmers don't quit in August; September is coming. Your due season has a date. Don't faint when you're this close. The difference between reaping and weeping is not fainting.

Reflection Question: Where are you closest to fainting that might be closest to harvest?

DAY 236

"And he said to his servant, Go up now, look toward the sea...And it came to pass at the seventh time, that he said, Behold, there ariseth a little cloud."
— *1 Kings 18:43-44 (KJV)*

Seven times the servant looked for rain. Six times, nothing. Imagine trip number five, climbing that mountain again, Elijah still praying, sky still clear. Most of us quit at trip three. But trip seven brought the cloud. What if your answer is on trip seven, but you stopped at six? Elijah heard rain before anyone saw clouds. He kept sending his servant because he knew what he heard. Your persistence might need to match what you've heard from God. The seventh look changed everything.

Reflection Question: What do you need to check for the seventh time?

DAY 237

"Persecuted, but not forsaken; cast down, but not destroyed." — *2 Corinthians 4:9 (KJV)*

Paul mastered the "but not" lifestyle. Persecuted BUT NOT forsaken. Cast down BUT NOT destroyed. The first part hurts; the second part heals. You might be knocked down, but you're not knocked out. That's endurance—taking hits but not staying hit. Every "but not" is a testimony. You're struggling but not sinking. Bent but not broken. Pressed but not crushed. The enemy can affect you but not destroy you. Your "but not" is your testimony.

Reflection Question: What's your "but not" testimony right now?

DAY 238

"I have fought a good fight, I have finished my course, I have kept the faith." — 2 Timothy 4:7 (KJV)

Paul didn't say he won every fight—he said he fought good. He didn't say his course was easy—he said he finished it. He didn't say faith was simple—he said he kept it. That's success: fighting, finishing, keeping. Your course isn't their course. Stop comparing your mile 5 to someone else's mile 20. Run your race, fight your fight, keep your faith. The goal isn't to be first; it's to finish. Paul's crown was for finishing, not winning.

Reflection Question: Are you running your race or comparing your pace?

DAY 239

"I returned, and saw under the sun, that the race is not to the swift, nor the battle to the strong...but time and chance happeneth to them all." — Ecclesiastes 9:11 (KJV)

The fastest doesn't always win. The strongest doesn't always conquer. Solomon says time and chance happen to everyone. Your timing might be off, but your time is coming. What looks like losing might just be waiting for your moment. That person who passed you might not finish. That opportunity you missed might not have been yours. Sometimes endurance beats speed. Sometimes patience beats power. Keep running—time and chance are still in play. The race isn't over until it's over.

Reflection Question: Where do you need to trust time and chance instead of speed and strength?

DAY 240

"O Lord, thou hast deceived me, and I was deceived...I am in derision daily, every one mocketh me." — Jeremiah 20:7 (KJV)

Even prophets want to quit. Jeremiah told God he felt tricked, mocked, ridiculed. But verse 9 says when he tried to quit, God's word became fire in his bones. He couldn't stop even when he wanted to. Your calling might feel like fire shut up in your bones—painful to carry, impossible to abort. Jeremiah teaches us it's okay to complain to God while continuing to obey. Endurance doesn't mean you don't struggle; it means you struggle forward. Fire in your bones won't let you quit.

Reflection Question: What fire in your bones won't let you quit despite the difficulty?

DAY 241

"Therefore, my beloved brethren, be ye stedfast, unmoveable, always abounding in the work of the Lord." — 1 Corinthians 15:58 (KJV)

Steadfast and unmoveable—that's the goal. Not excited and emotional, but steady and solid. The storm can blow, but you don't move. The trends can change, but you don't chase. You're anchored in something deeper than circumstances. "Always abounding"—not sometimes, not when you feel like it, but always. That's the kind of consistency that changes worlds. The person who shows up every day eventually shows up everyone who started strong but couldn't sustain. Consistency beats intensity over time.

Reflection Question: Where do you need to be more steadfast and less emotional?

DAY 242

"And the Lord thy God will put out those nations before thee by little and little." — Deuteronomy 7:22 (KJV)

God could have cleared Canaan instantly. Instead, He chose "little by little." Why? Verse 22 says if He did it all at once, wild beasts would multiply. Sometimes slow deliverance is protection. Your gradual victory might be God's wisdom. You want instant breakthrough, but God knows you need incremental growth. Little by little isn't lack of power; it's perfection of process. Each small victory prepares you for the next level. Trust the pace of "little by little."

Reflection Question: What "little by little" victory are you trying to rush?

DAY 243

"Let us hold fast the profession of our faith without wavering; (for he is faithful that promised)." — Hebrews 10:23 (KJV)

Hold fast—like gripping a rope while dangling over a cliff. Your profession of faith isn't casual confession; it's your lifeline. The parenthesis explains why: He who promised is faithful. Your grip might weaken, but His faithfulness doesn't. "Without wavering"—that's the challenge. No wobbling, no waffling, no wondering if you heard right. You did. Hold fast to what He said even when circumstances scream otherwise. His faithfulness is more reliable than your feelings. Your grip might be weak, but what you're gripping is unbreakable.

Reflection Question: What profession of faith do you need to hold fast without wavering?

SEPTEMBER: PEACE AND REST

DAY 244

"And he arose, and rebuked the wind, and said unto the sea, Peace, be still. And the wind ceased, and there was a great calm." — Mark 4:39 (KJV)

Jesus slept through the same storm that terrified seasoned fishermen. Think about that. Professional boat guys panicking while the carpenter naps. The difference? He knew who was really in control of the weather. When He finally woke up, He didn't grab a bucket or a sail. He spoke three words: "Peace, be still." The storm that was stronger than twelve grown men submitted to three words from Jesus. Your storm might be loud, but His voice is louder. The chaos you're trying to manage might just need you to wake up Jesus in your boat. He's not worried—He's resting, waiting for you to remember Who's with you.

Reflection Question: What storm are you trying to survive that Jesus could silence with a word?

DAY 245

"And he said unto them, The sabbath was made for man, and not man for the sabbath." — Mark 2:27 (KJV)

The Pharisees turned rest into rules. They made Sabbath harder than the work week. Jesus flipped it: Sabbath serves you, not vice versa. It's a gift, not a grade. God literally commanded you to take a day off, and you're treating it like extra credit. You feel guilty for resting while your phone buzzes with unfinished tasks. But God designed you to need rest. Your car needs oil changes, your phone needs charging, and you need Sabbath. It's not weakness—it's design. That seventh day isn't lazy; it's holy. Rest isn't the absence of productivity. It's the presence of peace.

Reflection Question: How have you turned God's gift of rest into a guilty obligation?

DAY 246

"But Martha was cumbered about much serving, and came to him, and said, Lord, dost thou not care that my sister hath left me to serve alone?" — Luke 10:40 (KJV)

Martha was making dinner for Jesus while Mary sat at His feet. Martha got mad—understandably. She's sweating in the kitchen while Mary's chilling in the living room. But Jesus said Mary chose better. Sometimes the spiritual thing looks lazy to the busy person. You're Martha, aren't you? Running around, serving everyone, getting irritated at people who aren't matching your pace. Meanwhile, you're missing Jesus in your own house because you're too busy serving Him to sit with Him. The meal can wait. His presence can't.

Reflection Question: What "serving" is keeping you from sitting with Jesus?

DAY 247

"He maketh me to lie down in green pastures: he leadeth me beside the still waters." — Psalm 23:2 (KJV)

Sheep don't lie down easily. They need to feel safe, satisfied, and free from friction in the flock. A sheep lying down in green pastures is a content sheep. David says God "makes" him lie down. Sometimes the Shepherd has to force rest on stubborn sheep. That forced slow-down—injury, job loss, pandemic—might be God making you lie down. You wouldn't choose rest, so He chose it for you. The green pastures were always there; you were just too driven to enjoy them. Still waters were flowing while you were frantically rushing. The Shepherd knows you need rest more than you need accomplishment.

Reflection Question: What situation is God using to make you lie down in green pastures?

DAY 248

"Be still, and know that I am God." — Psalm 46:10 (KJV)

Be still. In a world that rewards hustle, God says stop. Not forever, just long enough to remember who He is. Your frantic fixing might be interfering with His working. Sometimes the most powerful thing you can do is nothing. Stillness isn't empty—it's full of knowing. When you're still, you realize He's God and you're not. That's relieving, not insulting. The pressure you're carrying to make everything work? That's His job. Your job is to be still long enough to know that. Motion doesn't equal progress. Sometimes stillness is the strategy.

Reflection Question: What situation needs you to be still instead of busy?

DAY 249

"In Gibeon the Lord appeared to Solomon in a dream by night." — 1 Kings 3:5 (KJV)

God appeared to Solomon at night, in a dream, while he was sleeping. Not during his royal duties or religious ceremonies—during rest. Sometimes God waits until you're unconscious to speak because that's the only time you're quiet enough to hear. Your breakthrough might be hiding in your bedroom, not your boardroom. That answer you're chasing might come when you stop chasing. Solomon received history-changing wisdom while sleeping. Your rest isn't unproductive—it's receptive. Stop treating sleep like lost time. God's working the night shift.

Reflection Question: What might God be trying to tell you that requires rest to hear?

DAY 250

"Be careful for nothing; but in every thing by prayer and supplication with thanksgiving let your requests be made known unto God." — Philippians 4:6 (KJV)

"Careful for nothing" means anxious about nothing. Nothing. Not small things, not big things—nothing. Paul wrote this from prison, so he's not naive about problems. He's discovered something: anxiety accomplishes nothing, but prayer changes everything. You're anxious about stuff you can't control and stuff God already controls. That thing keeping you up at night? God's not losing sleep over it. Trade your anxiety for prayer. It's not denial—it's exchange. Give God your worry; take His peace. Anxiety is expensive. Peace is free.

Reflection Question: What anxiety needs to be converted to prayer?

DAY 251

"Come unto me, all ye that labour and are heavy laden, and I will give you rest." — Matthew 11:28 (KJV)

Jesus didn't say, "Come unto me, all ye who have it together." He invited the exhausted, the overwhelmed, the ones carrying too much. That's His target audience—people who need rest, not people who've mastered rest. You're trying to prove you can handle the load. Meanwhile, Jesus is offering to carry it. Not help you carry it—give you rest from it. But you have to come. Pride keeps you struggling; humility brings you rest. The load you're carrying wasn't meant for your shoulders.

Reflection Question: What burden do you need to bring to Jesus instead of bearing yourself?

DAY 252

"And as he lay and slept under a juniper tree, behold, then an angel touched him, and said unto him, Arise and eat." — 1 Kings 19:5 (KJV)

Elijah was suicidal, asking God to kill him. God's response? A nap and a meal. Not a sermon about faith, not a rebuke about doubt—sleep and food. Sometimes the most spiritual thing is the most practical thing. You're looking for deep spiritual solutions to what might be physical exhaustion. That depression might need rest more than revelation. That anger might need a sandwich more than a sermon. Elijah couldn't hear God until he rested and ate. God cares about your body, not just your soul.

Reflection Question: What spiritual problem might have a physical solution?

DAY 253

"And they came to him, and awoke him, saying, Master, master, we perish."
— Luke 8:24 (KJV)

The disciples woke Jesus with their panic. "We're dying!" He got up, handled the storm, then asked about their faith. He wasn't bothered by the storm—He was puzzled by their panic. They forgot who was in their boat. Your panic might be more concerning than your problem. The storm is real, but so is His presence. You're calculating survival odds based on your swimming ability, forgetting you have the Water-Walker aboard. Peace isn't about calm circumstances—it's about present Savior.

Reflection Question: How would your peace level change if you remembered Who's in your boat?

DAY 254

"Casting all your care upon him; for he careth for you." — *1 Peter 5:7 (KJV)*

Casting means throwing, not gently placing. Peter says throw your cares on God like you're getting rid of something heavy. Don't carefully hand them over—chuck them. This isn't polite; it's desperate. And God's okay with that. You're carrying cares like souvenirs, checking on them hourly to see if they've changed. Meanwhile, God's saying, "Throw those at Me. I care for you, so you don't have to care for yourself." It's a trade—your cares for His care. Stop curating your cares. Cast them.

Reflection Question: What care do you need to throw at God instead of carefully managing?

DAY 255

"And let us not be weary in well doing: for in due season we shall reap, if we faint not." — *Galatians 6:9 (KJV)*

Even good things can wear you out. Ministry, parenting, serving—all good, all exhausting. Paul acknowledges the weariness before promising the reward. It's normal to get tired doing right things. That's not weakness; that's humanity. The promise isn't that you won't get weary—it's that weariness isn't permanent. Due season is coming. The same good work that's wearing you out is producing a harvest you can't see yet. Don't let good exhaustion make you quit good work. Rest, don't resign.

Reflection Question: Where are you weary in well-doing that needs rest, not resignation?

DAY 256

"Except the Lord build the house, they labour in vain that build it...It is vain for you to rise up early, to sit up late, to eat the bread of sorrows." — *Psalm 127:1-2 (KJV)*

You're up before dawn, working past midnight, eating stress for breakfast. The psalmist calls it vain. Not lazy—vain. All that effort without God's involvement is just exhausting yourself for nothing. There's a difference between God-work and good work. One builds with heaven's blueprint; the other just builds. You might be constructing something God never ordained, wondering why you're so tired. Vain labor is exhausting because you're carrying weight God never assigned. Let God build, or you're just making noise with hammers.

Reflection Question: What are you building that God might not have blueprinted?

DAY 257

"Thou wilt keep him in perfect peace, whose mind is stayed on thee: because he trusteth in thee." — Isaiah 26:3 (KJV)

Perfect peace—not partial, not temporary, but perfect. The condition? A stayed mind. That means fixed, anchored, focused on God. Your mind wants to wander to worst-case scenarios, but peace comes from a stayed mind. It's like a camera focus. Whatever you focus on becomes clear while everything else blurs. Focus on problems, and they become overwhelming. Focus on God, and problems become blurry. Perfect peace isn't about perfect circumstances—it's about perfect focus. Your peace is proportional to your focus.

Reflection Question: What's stealing your focus from God and disrupting your peace?

DAY 258

"Return unto thy rest, O my soul; for the Lord hath dealt bountifully with thee." — Psalm 116:7 (KJV)

David talks to his own soul like it's a separate person. "Return to rest, soul. Remember what God's done." Sometimes you have to preach to yourself, remind yourself, redirect yourself back to rest. Your soul tends to wander from rest to worry. It needs regular redirection. "Soul, come back. God's been good. Remember? Rest in that." This isn't natural; it's intentional. Rest isn't where you drift—it's where you return. Talk to your soul before it talks to you.

Reflection Question: What does your soul need to be reminded of to return to rest?

DAY 259

"And when he had sent them away, he departed into a mountain to pray."
— *Mark 6:46 (KJV)*

After feeding five thousand, Jesus sent everyone away—even the disciples—and went alone to pray. At the height of ministry success, He chose solitude. He didn't network the miracle or maximize the momentum. He withdrew. You're afraid to withdraw because you might miss something. Jesus knew that withdrawing was how you don't miss everything. That mountain prayer time wasn't unproductive—it was restorative. Even Jesus needed alone time with the Father. If Jesus withdrew, why don't you?

Reflection Question: When did you last send everyone away to be alone with God?

DAY 260

"Now no chastening for the present seemeth to be joyous, but grievous: nevertheless afterward it yieldeth the peaceable fruit of righteousness." — *Hebrews 12:11 (KJV)*

Discipline doesn't feel peaceful—it feels painful. But the writer says "afterward" it yields peaceable fruit. Not during, but after. The correction that hurts now produces peace later. That's the trade-off. Your current discomfort might be producing future peace. That hard lesson, that difficult correction, that painful pruning—it's not pleasant, but it's productive. Peace isn't the absence of discipline; it's the result of it. Today's pain is tomorrow's peace.

Reflection Question: What current discipline is producing future peaceable fruit?

DAY 261

"For thus saith the Lord God, the Holy One of Israel; In returning and rest shall ye be saved; in quietness and in confidence shall be your strength." —
Isaiah 30:15 (KJV)

Your strength isn't in noise and activity—it's in quietness and confidence. That's counterintuitive. Everything in you wants to be loud and busy to feel strong. But God says real strength whispers and rests. Quiet confidence doesn't need to prove itself. It knows what it knows. While everyone else is shouting their strength, quiet confidence just is strong. Returning and rest save you, not running and rushing. Volume doesn't equal value. Quiet confidence speaks loudest.

Reflection Question: Where do you need quiet confidence instead of loud activity?

DAY 262

"It is vain for you to rise up early, to sit up late, to eat the bread of sorrows: for so he giveth his beloved sleep." — Psalm 127:2 (KJV)

The bread of sorrows—that's anxiety for breakfast, stress for lunch, worry for dinner. You're consuming concern like it's nourishment. Meanwhile, God gives His beloved sleep. Not insomnia, not anxiety—sleep. Sleep is a gift, not a waste. It's God's reset button for your soul. But you're treating it like the enemy of productivity. The bread of sorrows never satisfies; it just creates more hunger for worry. God feeds His beloved rest, not stress.

Reflection Question: What bread of sorrows are you eating instead of receiving sleep?

DAY 263

"O that thou hadst hearkened to my commandments! then had thy peace been as a river." — Isaiah 48:18 (KJV)

Rivers don't stop flowing because of rocks. They go over, around, or through. That's the peace God offers—not the absence of obstacles but the ability to flow despite them. River peace keeps moving. Your peace keeps depending on obstacle removal. God's peace flows regardless of rocks. If you'd listened to His commands, your peace would be riverlike—constant, flowing, unstoppable. It's not too late to start listening. Peace as a river doesn't mean no rocks—it means flowing anyway.

Reflection Question: What rocks are damming your river of peace?

DAY 264

"There remaineth therefore a rest to the people of God. For he that is entered into his rest, he also hath ceased from his own works." — Hebrews 4:9-10 (KJV)

There's a rest waiting that you haven't entered yet. Not because it's unavailable but because entering requires ceasing. Stop working for what's already finished. That's the rest God offers—not from work but from works. You're still trying to earn what's freely given. Still performing for acceptance that's already yours. God's rest comes when you cease from your own works—stop trying to save yourself, prove yourself, justify yourself. Rest remains for those who stop working for it.

Reflection Question: What works do you need to cease from to enter God's rest?

DAY 265

"To give unto them beauty for ashes, the oil of joy for mourning, the garment of praise for the spirit of heaviness." — *Isaiah 61:3 (KJV)*

Heaviness is like wearing a lead coat. Everything takes more effort. God offers a wardrobe change—garment of praise for spirit of heaviness. Not denial of heaviness but exchange of garments. Praise is a choice to change clothes. Take off heaviness; put on praise. It's not about feeling; it's about deciding. That spirit of heaviness wants to be your permanent outfit. But praise is available in your closet. You can't wear both garments. Choose.

Reflection Question: What heaviness do you need to exchange for praise?

DAY 266

"Whose mind is stayed on thee: because he trusteth in thee." — *Isaiah 26:3 (KJV)*

A stayed mind doesn't mean a perfect mind—it means an anchored one. Like a ship in harbor, anchored minds might feel waves but don't drift with them. The anchor isn't your strength; it's your trust. Your mind wants to drift with every current event, every what-if scenario. But trust anchors you to God's character, not circumstances. Stayed minds still feel storms; they just don't move with them. Trust is the anchor that creates the stay.

Reflection Question: What's causing your mind to drift from its anchor?

DAY 267

"For so he giveth his beloved sleep." — *Psalm 127:2 (KJV)*

Sleep is God's gift to His beloved. Not achievement, not productivity—sleep. You're beloved not because of what you accomplish awake but because of whose you are. And the beloved get sleep. Insomnia might be a trust issue. Can God handle the night shift? Can He work while you're unconscious? Your inability to sleep might reveal an inability to trust God with the controls. The beloved sleep because the Beloved never does.

Reflection Question: What's keeping you awake that God's already handling?

DAY 268

"Consider the lilies of the field, how they grow; they toil not, neither do they spin." — *Matthew 6:28 (KJV)*

Lilies don't have LinkedIn profiles. They don't network, hustle, or optimize. They just grow where planted and somehow end up more beautiful than Solomon's best outfit. There's a lesson in their laziness. You're toiling and spinning, trying to force growth. Meanwhile, lilies are teaching a masterclass in trust. They grow by being, not doing. Your constant motion might be preventing the growth that comes from stillness. Sometimes the most productive thing is photosynthesis, not progress.

Reflection Question: Where are you toiling and spinning instead of growing where planted?

DAY 269

"The Lord is my shepherd; I shall not want." — Psalm 23:1 (KJV)

Five words that change everything: "I shall not want." Not "might not" or "hopefully won't"—shall not. When the Lord is your shepherd, lack becomes impossible. You might not have everything, but you won't want anything. The difference between wanting and needing disappears under good shepherding. Sheep don't stress about tomorrow's grass because they trust today's shepherd. Your want list might be long, but with the Lord as shepherd, your needs are covered. Shepherded sheep don't stress about supply.

Reflection Question: What are you wanting that a good Shepherd would provide if needed?

DAY 270

"Grace and peace be multiplied unto you through the knowledge of God."
— 2 Peter 1:2 (KJV)

Peace can be multiplied, not just added. The multiplier? Knowledge of God. The more you know Him, the more exponential your peace becomes. It's mathematical—knowing God multiplies peace. You're trying to add peace through circumstances—a little here, a little there. But God offers multiplication through relationship. Every new thing you learn about God becomes a peace multiplier. Stop adding; start multiplying through knowing.

Reflection Question: What do you need to know about God that would multiply your peace?

DAY 271

"Yea, though I walk through the valley of the shadow of death, I will fear no evil." — Psalm 23:4 (KJV)

Even death valleys can be restful with the right Shepherd. David doesn't say "if I walk through"—he says "though I walk through." Valleys are guaranteed, but so is the Shepherd's presence. The valley of the shadow isn't the valley of death—it's just death's shadow. Shadows can't hurt you; they just look scary. With the Shepherd, even death's shadow becomes a walking path, not a camping ground. Rest is possible even in death's shadow.

Reflection Question: What valley shadow are you treating like actual death?

DAY 272

"Deep calleth unto deep at the noise of thy waterspouts: all thy waves and thy billows are gone over me." — Psalm 42:7 (KJV)

David felt overwhelmed—waves and billows going over, not around. But notice: "thy waves." Even the overwhelming stuff belongs to God. Your chaos isn't random; it's "thy waves." If they're His waves, He controls the tide. What feels like drowning might be divine deepening. The deep in you is calling to the deep in God. Sometimes you need waves to discover what depths you carry. Even overwhelming waves obey the One who owns them.

Reflection Question: What waves going over you need to be recognized as "thy waves"?

DAY 273

"Peace I leave with you, my peace I give unto you: not as the world giveth, give I unto you." — John 14:27 (KJV)

Jesus left peace like an inheritance. Not world peace—His peace. World peace depends on circumstances aligning. His peace exists despite circumstances. It's different inventory entirely. The world gives peace temporarily, conditionally, partially. Jesus gives peace permanently, unconditionally, completely. You keep shopping for world peace when Jesus already deposited His peace in your account. You have an inheritance of peace waiting to be claimed.

Reflection Question: Are you trying to earn world peace instead of receiving Christ's peace?

OCTOBER: GRATITUDE AND THANKSGIVING

DAY 274

"In every thing give thanks: for this is the will of God in Christ Jesus concerning you." — 1 Thessalonians 5:18 (KJV)

"In everything"—not "for everything." There's a difference. You're not thanking God for cancer, but you can thank Him in cancer. For betrayal? No. In betrayal? Yes. God doesn't expect you to be grateful for pain, but He knows gratitude in pain changes everything. It's like finding a twenty-dollar bill in your pocket during a bad day. The day's still bad, but now you've got pizza money. Gratitude in hardship doesn't erase the hardship—it just finds the hidden treasure. Your worst season might still contain something worth thanking God for. Gratitude isn't denial. It's detective work.

Reflection Question: What can you thank God for IN your current difficulty?

DAY 275

"And one of them, when he saw that he was healed, turned back, and with a loud voice glorified God." — Luke 17:15 (KJV)

Ten lepers healed. One came back. That's a 10% gratitude rate, and honestly, that might be generous for us. The other nine weren't ungrateful people—they were just excited about their new life. They forgot who gave it to them. You got the promotion, the healing, the breakthrough. Did you go back? Or did you run forward so fast you forgot to turn around and say thanks? That one leper became the story not because his healing was better but because his gratitude was visible. Sometimes the real miracle is remembering to say thanks.

Reflection Question: What healing have you received but haven't returned to give thanks for?

DAY 276

"He that regardeth the day, regardeth it unto the Lord; and he that regardeth not the day, to the Lord he doth not regard it. He that eateth, eateth to the Lord, for he giveth God thanks." — Romans 14:6 (KJV)

Paul says you can eat breakfast to God's glory just by saying thanks. That's it. Your scrambled eggs become worship with gratitude. Your coffee turns communion-ish. Ordinary becomes holy through thanksgiving. We're looking for massive ways to glorify God while missing the breakfast blessing. Every meal is three opportunities daily to practice gratitude. That's over a thousand chances per year to thank God, and you're waiting for something bigger? Your next meal is your next ministry opportunity.

Reflection Question: How would your meals change if you truly ate "to the Lord"?

DAY 277

"By him therefore let us offer the sacrifice of praise to God continually, that is, the fruit of our lips giving thanks to his name." — Hebrews 13:15 (KJV)

Sacrifice means it costs something. Praise when you don't feel like it—that's sacrifice. Thanks when you'd rather complain—that's offering. Your lips might not want to produce fruit of gratitude, but sacrifice doesn't wait for feelings. Old Testament folks brought dead animals. You bring living praise. Which is harder? Killing a lamb or praising through pain? Gratitude when life's good is reaction. Gratitude when life's garbage is sacrifice. Sometimes thanksgiving is the most expensive offering.

Reflection Question: What sacrifice of praise is hardest for you to offer right now?

DAY 278

"Then Job arose, and rent his mantle, and shaved his head, and fell down upon the ground, and worshipped." — Job 1:20 (KJV)

Job lost everything in one day. Kids, wealth, health—gone. His first response? Worship. Not after processing, not after counseling—immediately. He worshipped in the wreckage. That's next-level gratitude. "The Lord gave, and the Lord hath taken away; blessed be the name of the Lord." Job thanked God for the giving even in the taking. He remembered the blessing in the breaking. Your loss doesn't erase what you once had. Gratitude remembers the giving even during the grieving.

Reflection Question: What past giving can you thank God for despite present taking?

DAY 279

"Enter into his gates with thanksgiving, and into his courts with praise." — *Psalm 100:4 (KJV)*

Thanksgiving is the entry pass. You can't enter His gates grumpy. Gratitude is the key that opens God's presence. Not perfection, not performance—just thanks. That's the admission price. You're trying to enter through achievement or emotion. Meanwhile, the gate's waiting for gratitude. Simple thanks opens what complicated theology can't. Your grateful heart has more access than your perfect behavior. The password to His presence is "thank you."

Reflection Question: What gratitude do you need to offer to enter His gates?

DAY 280

"But I will sacrifice unto thee with the voice of thanksgiving; I will pay that that I have vowed." — *Jonah 2:9 (KJV)*

Jonah said this from inside a fish. Not after the beach, not once he showered—from inside the fish belly. He found something to be grateful for while marinating in stomach acid. That's professional-grade gratitude. Your situation stinks—maybe literally. But Jonah proves you can thank God from anywhere. Fish belly, jail cell, hospital bed, divorce court—thanksgiving travels. If Jonah can be grateful in gastric juice, you can be grateful in your situation. Location doesn't determine gratitude. Decision does.

Reflection Question: What can you thank God for from inside your "fish belly"?

DAY 281

"Now when Daniel knew that the writing was signed, he went into his house...and prayed, and gave thanks before his God, as he did aforetime."
— Daniel 6:10 (KJV)

Death sentence signed. Daniel's response? Same prayer routine, including thanks. He didn't skip gratitude because of the lions. He thanked God with execution looming. "As he did aforetime"—crisis didn't change his gratitude calendar. Your crisis wants to cancel your thanksgiving. Don't let it. Daniel proved gratitude isn't circumstantial. It's habitual. He gave thanks facing lions because he gave thanks every normal Tuesday too. Consistent gratitude survives crisis.

Reflection Question: What thanksgiving habit continues regardless of your circumstances?

DAY 282

"And at midnight Paul and Silas prayed, and sang praises unto God: and the prisoners heard them." — *Acts 16:25 (KJV)*

Blood on their backs, feet in stocks, maximum security prison. Midnight. They sang. Not quietly—the other prisoners heard them. That's gratitude with volume. Their praise concert confused everyone because it didn't match their condition. Your midnight might need a song. Not because you feel musical but because gratitude at midnight is warfare. Other prisoners are listening. Your praise in prison might be their introduction to freedom. Midnight gratitude has an audience you don't see.

Reflection Question: What midnight deserves a praise song?

DAY 283

"And when he had given thanks, he brake it, and said, Take, eat: this is my body." — 1 Corinthians 11:24 (KJV)

Jesus gave thanks before breaking. He thanked God for bread about to be broken—His body about to be crucified. He modeled gratitude before suffering, not just after survival. You want to thank God after the breaking ends. Jesus thanked Him before it began. Anticipatory gratitude—thanking God for what hasn't happened yet, even when what's coming hurts. Can you thank God for bread that's about to break?

Reflection Question: What future breaking needs present thanking?

DAY 284

"For every creature of God is good, and nothing to be refused, if it be received with thanksgiving." — 1 Timothy 4:4 (KJV)

Thanksgiving sanctifies everything. That job you hate becomes good when received with thanks. That singleness you're enduring, that city you're stuck in—thanksgiving transforms them from refused to received. Paul says "nothing to be refused if received with thanksgiving." Gratitude is alchemy—it turns lead into gold. Not by changing the thing but by changing your reception of it. Thanksgiving makes everything receivable.

Reflection Question: What have you been refusing that needs receiving with thanksgiving?

DAY 285

"O magnify the Lord with me, and let us exalt his name together." — Psalm 34:3 (KJV)

David didn't want to magnify alone. Gratitude multiplies in community. Your thanks plus my thanks equals more than two thanks. That's gratitude math—it compounds when shared. You're keeping your gratitude private, but David says make it public. Invite others into your thanksgiving. Your testimony of gratitude might unlock someone else's. Magnifying together makes the magnificent more visible. Gratitude is contagious. Spread it.

Reflection Question: Who do you need to invite to magnify the Lord with you?

DAY 286

"Bless the Lord, O my soul, and forget not all his benefits." — Psalm 103:2 (KJV)

David talks to his soul again: "Don't forget!" Because souls have amnesia about benefits. You remember the wounds but forget the healing. Remember the lack but forget the provision. Gratitude requires intentional remembering. Make a list. Seriously. What benefits has your forgetful soul dropped? That close call you survived, that provision that appeared, that person who stayed—your soul forgot. Gratitude is partly memory work. Forgetting benefits is expensive. Remember.

Reflection Question: What benefits does your soul need to remember?

DAY 287

"Let the peace of God rule in your hearts...and be ye thankful." — *Colossians 3:15 (KJV)*

Peace and gratitude are roommates. Where one lives, the other moves in. You can't be grateful and anxious simultaneously. Try it. Thank God while panicking. Doesn't work. Gratitude evicts anxiety. "Be ye thankful"—it's a command, not a suggestion. God's not hoping you'll feel grateful. He's commanding gratitude regardless of feelings. Because He knows gratitude changes the heart's climate. Thankfulness is a thermostat, not a thermometer.

Reflection Question: What anxiety needs evicting through gratitude?

DAY 288

"It is of the Lord's mercies that we are not consumed, because his compassions fail not. They are new every morning." — *Lamentations 3:22-23 (KJV)*

Jeremiah wrote this during Jerusalem's destruction. The city's burning, people are starving, and he finds fresh mercy every morning. That's professional gratitude—finding new compassion in old rubble. Every morning delivers fresh mercy. Like manna, it doesn't keep overnight. Yesterday's mercy expired at midnight. But dawn brought new inventory. You woke up to fresh compassion you haven't even unwrapped yet. Morning mercy deserves morning gratitude.

Reflection Question: What new mercy came with this morning?

DAY 289

"As ye have therefore received Christ Jesus the Lord, so walk ye in him...abounding therein with thanksgiving." — Colossians 2:6-7 (KJV)

Abounding means overflowing, excessive, more than necessary. Not polite thanksgiving but abounding thanksgiving. The kind that makes people uncomfortable. The gratitude that seems disproportionate to your situation. You received Christ—everything else is bonus. That alone deserves abounding thanks. But you're portioning out gratitude like it's expensive. Abounding thanksgiving doesn't measure; it floods. Stop rationing gratitude. Abound.

Reflection Question: Where does your thanksgiving need to shift from measured to abounding?

DAY 290

"Let us come before his presence with thanksgiving, and make a joyful noise unto him with psalms." — Psalm 95:2 (KJV)

Thanksgiving is the pre-game for presence. You enter His presence through the door of gratitude. It's the warm-up act for worship. You can't skip thanksgiving and jump to requests. Make a joyful noise—it doesn't have to be pretty. God prefers off-key gratitude over on-point grumbling. Your thanksgiving might sound rough, but it sounds beautiful to heaven. Noisy gratitude beats silent resentment.

Reflection Question: What joyful noise of thanksgiving does God want to hear?

DAY 291

"Offer unto God thanksgiving; and pay thy vows unto the most High." —
Psalm 50:14 (KJV)

Thanksgiving is an offering, not just an attitude. You bring it like sacrifice, intentionally, costly. What thanksgiving are you withholding because it costs too much pride? That thanks you owe but don't want to give—that's the expensive offering God wants. Thanking Him for the thing you didn't want but needed. That's sacrificial gratitude. Some thanksgiving costs everything.

Reflection Question: What costly thanksgiving do you need to offer?

DAY 292

"And he took the seven loaves and the fishes, and gave thanks, and brake them." — *Matthew 15:36 (KJV)*

Jesus gave thanks for insufficient resources. Seven loaves, few fish, four thousand men plus families. The math didn't work, but gratitude did. He thanked God for not enough, then distributed more than enough. Your insufficient might be waiting for gratitude to multiply it. Thank God for the little that shouldn't be enough. Gratitude might be the ingredient that triggers multiplication. Thank God for insufficient and watch it become infinite.

Reflection Question: What insufficient resource needs gratitude to multiply?

DAY 293

"Not that I speak in respect of want: for I have learned, in whatsoever state I am, therewith to be content." — Philippians 4:11 (KJV)

Paul learned contentment—it wasn't natural. Prison taught him. Shipwrecks schooled him. Beatings built it. Contentment is curriculum, and gratitude is how you graduate. You're waiting for better circumstances to be grateful. Paul says be grateful in these circumstances. Contentment isn't about having enough; it's about thanking God for what you have. Gratitude teaches contentment.

Reflection Question: What current state needs gratitude to create contentment?

DAY 294

"And thou shalt remember that thou wast a bondman in the land of Egypt, and the Lord thy God redeemed thee." — Deuteronomy 15:15 (KJV)

Remember where you came from. You were a slave—to sin, addiction, fear, whatever. Remember the bondage to appreciate the freedom. Gratitude has memory. You've forgotten your Egypt. The bondage seems distant, so freedom feels normal. But normal for you was slavery until God intervened. Remember your redemption story. Gratitude remembers the pit to appreciate the palace.

Reflection Question: What bondage do you need to remember to fuel gratitude?

DAY 295

"Giving thanks always for all things unto God and the Father in the name of our Lord Jesus Christ." — Ephesians 5:20 (KJV)

Always. All things. Paul doesn't do halfway. Not selected things, not sometimes—always for all. That includes the stuff you wouldn't choose, the people you wouldn't pick, the path you wouldn't plan. This isn't toxic positivity. It's recognizing God's sovereignty in all things. Even the hard things serve purposes. Thank God for all means all—the bitter and sweet. Selective gratitude isn't full gratitude.

Reflection Question: What "all things" have you excluded from thanksgiving?

DAY 296

"Oh that men would praise the Lord for his goodness, and for his wonderful works to the children of men!" — Psalm 107:8 (KJV)

The psalmist wishes out loud that people would praise out loud. Silent gratitude is better than nothing, but vocal thanks is better than silence. God's goodness deserves volume. You're thinking thanks but not saying it. Your gratitude is on mute while your complaints have surround sound. Flip the audio. Let thanksgiving be louder than grumbling. Gratitude needs voice, not just thought.

Reflection Question: What thanksgiving needs to move from thought to throat?

DAY 297

"I beseech you therefore, brethren, by the mercies of God, that ye present your bodies a living sacrifice." — Romans 12:1 (KJV)

Because of God's mercies—that's why you sacrifice. Gratitude motivates offering. You present yourself not to earn mercy but because mercy was already given. Living sacrifice means daily dying, daily offering, daily gratitude. Not a one-time altar moment but continual presentation. Your gratitude keeps you on the altar. Mercy received demands life offered.

Reflection Question: How does gratitude for God's mercy motivate your living sacrifice?

DAY 298

"They that go down to the sea in ships, that do business in great waters...They cry unto the Lord in their trouble, and he bringeth them out of their distresses." — Psalm 107:23,28 (KJV)

Sailors know storms. They also know deliverance. The psalm says they cried; He delivered. Their gratitude comes from experience—they've been in storms and seen salvation. Your storms qualified you for deeper gratitude. People who've never been seasick can't appreciate solid ground like you can. Your troubles became your testimony. Storm survivors have the best gratitude stories.

Reflection Question: What storm deliverance needs to become a gratitude testimony?

DAY 299

"But he giveth more grace. Wherefore he saith, God resisteth the proud, but giveth grace unto the humble." — James 4:6 (KJV)

More grace. Not just grace—more grace. God's not rationing. But notice the condition: humility. Pride blocks grace; gratitude acknowledges it. Every thanks is humility admitting, "I didn't do this myself." You want more grace? More gratitude creates capacity. Thanksgiving is humility in action, and humility attracts grace. Pride repels what gratitude attracts. Grateful hearts get grace refills.

Reflection Question: Where does pride need replacing with grateful humility?

DAY 300

"Then sang Moses and the children of Israel this song unto the Lord, and spake, saying, I will sing unto the Lord, for he hath triumphed gloriously." — Exodus 15:1 (KJV)

They're on the beach, Egypt's army floating behind them, and they break into song. Not planning committee, not strategy session—concert. Their first act of freedom was gratitude. Your breakthrough might need a song before a strategy. Thank God for the deliverance before figuring out the desert. Moses knew—gratitude first, planning second. Sing on your beach before entering your wilderness.

Reflection Question: What deliverance deserves a song before strategy?

DAY 301

"And Hannah prayed, and said, My heart rejoiceth in the Lord, mine horn is exalted in the Lord." — 1 Samuel 2:1 (KJV)

Hannah prayed for years for a son. When Samuel came, her prayer was pure gratitude. Not requests for his future, not worry about raising him—just thanks. She even gave him back to God in gratitude. Your long-awaited answer might need more thanks and less analysis. Hannah shows us that gratitude for answered prayer should exceed the original desperation. Thank louder than you asked.

Reflection Question: What answered prayer needs louder thanks?

DAY 302

"Thou crownest the year with thy goodness; and thy paths drop fatness." — Psalm 65:11 (KJV)

The year gets crowned with goodness. Looking back, can you see the crown? The paths dripping with fatness (abundance)? Your year might have felt lean, but God's been dropping provision along your path. October means harvest. Time to count crops, not just costs. What grew this year that you haven't noticed because you're focused on what died? Every year wears a crown if you look for it.

Reflection Question: What crown of goodness has this year worn?

DAY 303

"When I remember thee upon my bed, and meditate on thee in the night watches." — Psalm 63:6 (KJV)

David's insomnia became intercession. When sleep wouldn't come, gratitude did. Those 2 AM wake-ups might be gratitude appointments. Instead of counting sheep, count blessings. Your night watches could become thanksgiving watches. That brain that won't shut off—redirect it to remembrance. Meditate on God's goodness instead of tomorrow's problems. Insomnia might be invitation to gratitude.

Reflection Question: How could your sleepless nights become thanksgiving watches?

DAY 304

"He delivered me from my strong enemy, and from them which hated me: for they were too strong for me." — Psalm 18:17 (KJV)

David admits—they were too strong for him. His gratitude comes from recognizing he should have lost. The enemy was stronger, but God was strongest. Deliverance from superior enemies deserves superior gratitude. What enemy was too strong for you but not for God? That addiction, depression, situation that should have won—it didn't. You're here because God delivered. Impossible victories demand intentional gratitude.

Reflection Question: What too-strong enemy did God deliver you from?

NOVEMBER: HOPE AND HEALING

DAY 305

"And he said unto them, Why are ye troubled? and why do thoughts arise in your hearts? Behold my hands and my feet, that it is I myself." — Luke 24:38-39 (KJV)

Jesus could have come back without scars. He's God—perfect healing was an option. But He kept them. Showed them off, actually. "Look, it's really me. Here's the proof." His scars became His ID. Your scars embarrass you. That bankruptcy, that divorce, that addiction recovery—you hide them like guilty secrets. But what if they're your testimony? Jesus didn't come back pretending crucifixion never happened. He came back proving He survived it. Your scars say the same thing: "I'm still here." The disciples recognized Him by His wounds, not His perfection. People might recognize Jesus in you the same way.

Reflection Question: Which scar are you hiding that could be someone else's hope?

DAY 306

"And he said unto me, Son of man, can these bones live? And I answered, O Lord God, thou knowest." — Ezekiel 37:3 (KJV)

God asked Ezekiel a ridiculous question while standing in a graveyard of bones: "Can these live?" Ezekiel's smart answer: "You tell me, God." That marriage reduced to bones. That dream buried years ago. That relationship past saving. God asks you the same question: "Can it live?" Science says no. Experience says no. But God specializes in impossible resurrections. Ezekiel spoke to bones, and they became an army. Maybe your dead situation just needs someone bold enough to speak life.

Reflection Question: What valley of bones is God asking you to speak life over?

DAY 307

"And a woman having an issue of blood twelve years, which had spent all that she had upon physicians, neither could be healed of any." — Luke 8:43 (KJV)

Twelve years. That's 4,380 days of disappointment. She tried everything, spent everything, and got nothing. Every doctor said the same: "Sorry, can't help you." But then she heard about Jesus and thought, "One more try." You've been in the waiting room so long they know your coffee order. Every treatment has failed. Hope feels risky after so much heartbreak. But what if the next touch is the one? She broke past crowds—and rules—and twelve years ended with one reach. Yours could too.

Reflection Question: What twelve-year problem needs one more faith-reach?

DAY 308

"And ought not this woman, being a daughter of Abraham, whom Satan hath bound, lo, these eighteen years, be loosed from this bond on the sabbath day?" — Luke 13:16 (KJV)

Eighteen years bent over. She could only see dirt and feet. Then Jesus showed up at church on Saturday and the religious folks got mad He healed her. They preferred their rules to her relief. Some of you have been bent over so long, you've forgotten what the sky looks like. Depression, shame, or sickness has kept your eyes down for years. And maybe some religious voice is saying healing can't happen now, today, for you. Jesus disagrees. He called her "daughter of Abraham"—gave her identity before healing. You're not just your problem. You're a child of promise, bent over maybe, but about to stand tall.

Reflection Question: What eighteen-year bend is ready to be straightened?

DAY 309

"Who remembered us in our low estate: for his mercy endureth for ever." — Psalm 136:23 (KJV)

"Low estate"—that's Bible-speak for rock bottom. The psalmist says God remembered us there. Not after we climbed out, not when we got it together—in the low estate. His memory works best when we're at our worst. Rock bottom has an address, and God knows it. He's got GPS to your lowest point. That place where you think nobody can find you? He remembers you there. His mercy has your coordinates. You're not lost; you're located. Not forgotten; remembered. The low estate is still in God's neighborhood.

Reflection Question: How is God remembering you in your current low estate?

DAY 310

"He saith unto him the third time, Simon, son of Jonas, lovest thou me?" —
John 21:17 (KJV)

Three denials. Three restorations. Jesus didn't replace Peter; He restored him. Most of us would have found a new disciple, someone without the betrayal baggage. Jesus chose rehabilitation over replacement. Peter thought his ministry ended at that campfire. One moment of fear seemed to erase three years of following. But Jesus cooked breakfast on another fire and rewrote the story. Your failure might feel final, but Jesus specializes in second acts. Notice Jesus didn't bring it up once and move on. Three times He asked, three times Peter answered. Full restoration takes time.

Reflection Question: What three-time failure needs three-time restoration?

DAY 311

"Jesus said, Take ye away the stone. Martha, the sister of him that was dead, saith unto him, Lord, by this time he stinketh: for he hath been dead four days." — *John 11:39 (KJV)*

Martha tried to protect Jesus from the smell of death. "It's been four days. This is going to be bad." She was being practical. Death stinks—literally. But Jesus wasn't worried about the odor. Your situation might stink. Really stink. The marriage is four days dead, the career is decomposing, the dream is past fresh. Everyone can smell the death. But Jesus stands at tombs and says, "Roll away the stone anyway." Sometimes hope means ignoring the stench and believing resurrection is stronger than rot.

Reflection Question: What four-day-dead situation needs the stone rolled away?

DAY 312

"And many charged him that he should hold his peace: but he cried the more a great deal, Thou son of David, have mercy on me." — Mark 10:48 (KJV)

Everyone told him to shut up. "Jesus is too important for your problems." But Bartimaeus got louder. Desperate people don't do polite. When you need healing badly enough, you stop caring what people think. The crowd wanted him quiet, but Jesus wanted him close. Your desperation might embarrass everyone except the One who matters. They say you're too loud, too needy, too much. Jesus says, "What do you want me to do?" Sometimes healing requires ignoring the shushers and shouting louder.

Reflection Question: What cry for help are you muffling to keep others comfortable?

DAY 313

"And he arose, and came to his father. But when he was yet a great way off, his father saw him, and had compassion, and ran." — Luke 15:20 (KJV)

The father ran. Dignified Middle Eastern fathers didn't run, but this one did. He'd been watching that road, hoping. Every distant figure might be his boy. Then one day, it was. You've been in the pigpen so long, you think you smell permanent. The rehearsed apology feels hollow. "He won't take me back, not after this." But the Father's been watching your road. He's not waiting for you to get close enough to smell; He's running while you're still distant. The journey home is shorter than you think when the Father's running toward you.

Reflection Question: What road is the Father watching, waiting for you to start walking?

DAY 314

*"And the Lord turned the captivity of Job, when he prayed for his friends:
also the Lord gave Job twice as much as he had before." — Job 42:10 (KJV)*

Job's restoration started when he prayed for the friends who
failed him. The guys who kicked him while he was down, who
preached when they should have been silent—Job prayed for
them. That's when everything turned. Your breakthrough
might be waiting for you to pray for the people who hurt you
during your breakdown. Not fair? No. But blessing those who
failed you might unlock your own blessing. Job got double
back, but first he had to forgive forward. Sometimes healing
starts with praying for the people who made it worse.

*Reflection Question: Which friend who failed you needs your
prayers?*

DAY 315

*"And when he was in affliction, he besought the Lord his God, and humbled
himself greatly before the God of his fathers." — 2 Chronicles 33:12 (KJV)*

Manasseh was the worst king Judah ever had. Child sacrifice, witchcraft, idolatry—he did it all. Then he got captured,
chained, and desperate. From prison, the worst king prayed,
and God heard him. Let that sink in. If God heard Manasseh,
He'll hear you. Your sins might be serious, but they're not
child-sacrifice serious. Manasseh proves nobody's too far
gone. Prison became his prayer closet, chains became his
chances. He humbled himself "greatly"—matching his great sin
with great humility. The worst king became proof that God's
mercy is greater than your mess.

*Reflection Question: What "Manasseh-level" mess makes you
think you're beyond mercy?*

DAY 316

"I have heard thy prayer, I have seen thy tears: behold, I will heal thee...And I will add unto thy days fifteen years." — *2 Kings 20:5-6 (KJV)*

Hezekiah was supposed to die. Isaiah said so. Death was scheduled, confirmed, prophet-approved. But Hezekiah turned his face to the wall and changed God's mind with tears. Fifteen bonus years because he cried and prayed. Your death sentence might not be final. That diagnosis, that deadline, that "definite" ending—what if tears could change it? Hezekiah didn't accept Isaiah's timeline. He appealed to a higher court. God saw his tears and rewrote his calendar. Sometimes healing comes through holy arguing with heaven's timeline.

Reflection Question: What "final" verdict needs appealing through tears and prayer?

DAY 317

"And they come to Jesus, and see him that was possessed with the devil, and had the legion, sitting, and clothed, and in his right mind." — *Mark 5:15 (KJV)*

From graveyard to clothed and calm. From chains to conversation. Legion went from horror movie to testimony in one encounter. The town was terrified—not of the old him, but the new him. Change that dramatic scares people. Your transformation might frighten folks who got comfortable with your dysfunction. They knew how to handle your demons; they don't know what to do with your deliverance. Sitting clothed in your right mind after years of chaos—that's scarier to some than your screaming was. Dramatic healing disturbs people who prefer predictable problems.

Reflection Question: Whose comfort with your dysfunction might be threatened by your deliverance?

DAY 318

"But Naaman was wroth, and went away, and said, Behold, I thought, He will surely come out to me, and stand, and call on the name of the Lord." —
2 Kings 5:11 (KJV)

Naaman wanted dramatic healing—prophet appearances, spectacular ceremonies. Instead, he got "go wash in the muddy river seven times." He almost missed his miracle because it didn't match his expectations. Your healing might not be Instagram-worthy. It might be mundane, repetitive, humbling. Seven dips in muddy water. Taking the medication. Going to counseling. Saying sorry. Again. The spectacular healing you want might be hiding in the simple obedience you're avoiding. Pride almost cost Naaman his skin. Literally.

Reflection Question: What simple healing instruction are you rejecting because it's not spectacular?

DAY 319

"And when they could not come nigh unto him for the press, they uncovered the roof where he was: and when they had broken it up, they let down the bed." — Mark 2:4 (KJV)

They destroyed someone's roof to get their friend to Jesus. Property damage for the sake of healing. These friends didn't let crowds, conventions, or ceilings stop them. They literally broke through barriers. Your healing might require friends willing to tear up some roofs. Or you might need to be that friend. Sometimes faith looks like property damage in pursuit of miracles. Those four friends probably got sued, but their paralyzed friend walked home. Hope sometimes requires holy vandalism.

Reflection Question: What roof needs removing to get someone to Jesus?

DAY 320

"And David said unto him, Fear not: for I will surely shew thee kindness for Jonathan thy father's sake, and will restore thee all the land of Saul." — 2 Samuel 9:7 (KJV)

Mephibosheth was dropped as a baby, crippled for life, hiding in Lo-debar (literally "no pasture"). Then David found him and brought him to the royal table. From forgotten to family. From nobody to nobility. You might be hiding in your own Lo-debar, convinced your damage disqualifies you. Dropped by people who should have held you, crippled by circumstances, living in "no pasture." But the King is looking for you, not to punish but to promote. Your limp doesn't disqualify you from the table.

Reflection Question: What Lo-debar are you hiding in that the King wants to rescue you from?

DAY 321

"And he looked up, and said, I see men as trees, walking." — Mark 8:24 (KJV)

First touch: blurry vision. Trees walking around. Not perfect healing, but better than blindness. Jesus touched him again for complete clarity. Sometimes healing happens in stages, not instantly. You might be in the "trees walking" stage—better but not best, improved but not ideal. That's not failed healing; it's progressive healing. Don't settle for trees when you're meant to see clearly, but don't despise partial progress either. The fact that you see trees walking means you're between blindness and sight.

Reflection Question: What area of your life is in the "trees walking" stage of healing?

DAY 322

"And, behold, there was a woman which had a spirit of infirmity eighteen years, and was bowed together, and could in no wise lift up herself." — *Luke 13:11 (KJV)*

Eighteen years studying floors. She knew every crack in every pavement. "Could in no wise lift up herself"—she tried everything. Then Jesus called her "daughter of Abraham" and suddenly she stood straight. Some conditions require divine intervention. You've tried every self-help book, every program, every prescription. Still bent. That's not failure; that's preparation for a miracle. When you can "in no wise" fix yourself, you're positioned for Jesus to fix you. Eighteen years ended in an instant. Yours might too.

Reflection Question: What eighteen-year bend have you been unable to straighten yourself?

DAY 323

"Who had his dwelling among the tombs; and no man could bind him, no, not with chains." — *Mark 5:3 (KJV)*

He was too strong for chains but not stronger than his demons. Living among the dead, screaming at mountains, cutting himself with stones. The whole town gave up on him. Then Jesus showed up in his graveyard. Maybe you're too strong for human help but not strong enough to free yourself. Living among dead things—dead relationships, dead dreams, dead hope. The chains meant to help just made it worse. But Jesus visits graveyards looking for people like you. Too strong for chains doesn't mean too far for Christ.

Reflection Question: What graveyard have you been living in that Jesus wants to visit?

DAY 324

"And the angel of the Lord appeared unto him, and said unto him, The Lord is with thee, thou mighty man of valour." — Judges 6:12 (KJV)

God called Gideon mighty while he was hiding in a wine press, threshing wheat in fear. That's either cruel sarcasm or prophetic declaration. God doesn't call you what you are; He calls you what you're becoming. You're hiding from your problems, and God's calling you mighty. You feel like a coward; He sees a warrior. The wine press is just where you are, not who you are. Your hiding place might be where God announces your hero status. Mighty men sometimes start in wine presses.

Reflection Question: What is God calling you that contradicts where you're hiding?

DAY 325

"That I may know him, and the power of his resurrection, and the fellowship of his sufferings." — Philippians 3:10 (KJV)

Paul wanted resurrection power AND suffering fellowship. You can't have one without the other. The same power that raises also relates to pain. Easter only makes sense after Friday. Your suffering isn't separate from resurrection—it's preparation for it. The depth of your pain is creating capacity for power. You're in fellowship with His sufferings, which means you're qualified for resurrection power. The tomb is temporary when resurrection power is available.

Reflection Question: How is your current suffering preparing you for resurrection power?

DAY 326

"Now there cried a certain woman of the wives of the sons of the prophets unto Elisha, saying, Thy servant my husband is dead; and thou knowest that thy servant did fear the Lord: and the creditor is come." — 2 Kings 4:1 (KJV)

Widow. Debt. Creditors threatening her sons. Rock, meet bottom. Elisha asked what she had. "Nothing but a pot of oil." That "nothing but" became everything when God got involved. Your "nothing but" might be enough—small skills or resources you think are insignificant. In God's hands, "nothing but" can overflow. She poured until she ran out of vessels, not God's provision. "Nothing but" plus God is always more than enough.

Reflection Question: What "nothing but" do you have that God could multiply?

DAY 327

"And he took the damsel by the hand, and said unto her, Talitha cumi; which is, being interpreted, Damsel, I say unto thee, arise." — Mark 5:41 (KJV)

Twelve years old. Dead. Mourners already hired. Jesus said she was sleeping; they laughed. He kicked out everyone except parents and three disciples. Sometimes healing requires removing the crowd. Your situation might have too many voices. The mourners are already performing, declaring death final. But Jesus speaks different languages than mourners. "Little lamb, get up." That's what Talitha cumi means—intimate, gentle, powerful. Death was interrupting her childhood. Jesus interrupted death.

Reflection Question: What premature death needs Jesus to speak "arise" over?

DAY 328

"And when she came to the man of God to the hill, she caught him by the feet...And she said, It is well." — 2 Kings 4:27-26 (KJV)

Her son was dead on her bed. When asked if everything was okay, she said, "It is well." That's not denial—that's defiant faith. She refused to speak death while seeking life. "It is well" while carrying catastrophe—that's professional-level hope. She didn't update her Facebook status to "devastated." She held her tragedy silent until she reached the solution. Sometimes hope means not announcing death while pursuing resurrection. What you say while seeking miracles matters.

Reflection Question: What death are you speaking over that needs "it is well" instead?

DAY 329

"He restoreth my soul: he leadeth me in the paths of righteousness for his name's sake." — Psalm 23:3 (KJV)

Restore means return to original condition. David's soul needed restoration—the man after God's heart needed repair. If David needed restoration, your need doesn't disqualify you. Souls get damaged. Life dents them, sin stains them, disappointment drains them. But the Shepherd specializes in soul restoration. Not replacement—restoration. He's not trading you in for a newer model. He's restoring your original design. Damaged souls are still valuable to the Shepherd.

Reflection Question: What part of your soul needs restoring to original condition?

DAY 330

"And one of them, when he saw that he was healed, turned back, and with a loud voice glorified God, And fell down on his face at his feet, giving him thanks: and he was a Samaritan." — Luke 17:15-16 (KJV)

Ten healed. One returned. And he was the "wrong" nationality—a Samaritan. Sometimes outsiders understand healing better than insiders. He came back loud, grateful, face-down worship. Your healing isn't complete until you've returned to say thanks. The other nine got skin restoration; this one got soul transformation. He was healed going, but made whole by returning. There's a difference between healed and whole. Gratitude completes what healing starts.

Reflection Question: What healing needs completing through returning to give thanks?

DAY 331

"And so will I go in unto the king, which is not according to the law: and if I perish, I perish." — Esther 4:16 (KJV)

Esther risked death to prevent genocide. "If I perish, I perish"—that's courage calculating cost and proceeding anyway. Her people's healing required her willingness to die. Your breakthrough might require similar risk. Not physical death, maybe, but death to comfort, reputation, security. "If I perish, I perish" is the prayer of people who value purpose over preservation. Sometimes healing a nation starts with one person's risky obedience.

Reflection Question: What "if I perish, I perish" risk is your healing waiting for?

DAY 332

"And lest I should be exalted above measure through the abundance of the revelations, there was given to me a thorn in the flesh." — 2 Corinthians 12:7 (KJV)

Three times Paul begged for healing. Three times God said, "My grace is sufficient." Some thorns are teachers. Not every problem gets removed; some get redeemed. Paul's weakness became his strange strength. Your thorn might be permanent but purposeful. That thing you've prayed away repeatedly—what if it's keeping you humble, dependent, useful? Not all healing looks like removal. Sometimes it looks like grace to endure. Thorns with purpose hurt differently than pointless pain.

Reflection Question: What thorn might God be using rather than removing?

DAY 333

"Multitudes, multitudes in the valley of decision: for the day of the Lord is near in the valley of decision." — Joel 3:14 (KJV)

The valley of decision is crowded. Everyone's there eventually—that place where you must choose: hope or despair, faith or fear, healing or hiding. The valley won't let you stay neutral. Your healing might be waiting for your decision. Not God's decision—He already chose healing. Your decision to believe, receive, act. The valley of decision is where maybe becomes yes or no. Multitudes are in the valley. But your decision is singular.

Reflection Question: What decision is your valley waiting for?

DAY 334

"For I know the thoughts that I think toward you, saith the Lord, thoughts of peace, and not of evil, to give you an expected end." — Jeremiah 29:11 (KJV)

God's thinking about you. Right now. And His thoughts are peaceful, not punishing. He's planning your expected end—literally, your hope-filled future. Written from captivity to captives, this promise proves location doesn't determine destination. You might be in Babylon, but God's thoughts are about your future, not your failure. His plans survived your mistakes. Your expected end is still expected, still ending well. God's thoughts about you are better than your thoughts about yourself.

Reflection Question: How would believing God's thoughts about you change your hope level?

December: Joy and Celebration

Day 335

"And David danced before the Lord with all his might; and David was girded with a linen ephod." — 2 Samuel 6:14 (KJV)

The king in his underwear, basically, dancing like nobody's watching. His wife was mortified. David didn't care. The ark was coming home, and dignity took a backseat to joy. Sometimes celebration requires looking foolish. When did you last dance before the Lord? Not literally, maybe (or maybe literally), but when did joy override your dignity? David said he'd become even more undignified if it meant celebrating God properly. Your joy might be waiting for you to stop caring what people think.

Reflection Question: What would you celebrate if dignity wasn't a concern?

DAY 336

"And Mary said, My soul doth magnify the Lord, And my spirit hath rejoiced in God my Saviour." — Luke 1:46-47 (KJV)

Pregnant teenager, unwed, facing scandal. Her response? Magnificat—one of the most beautiful songs in Scripture. She found joy in the midst of what should have been shame. That's professional-level celebration. Mary teaches us that joy doesn't wait for perfect circumstances. She rejoiced while morning sickness probably raged, while people definitely whispered. Her spirit rejoiced despite her situation. She magnified God, not her problems. Your magnificat might be waiting in your mess.

Reflection Question: What difficult situation contains hidden reasons to magnify God?

DAY 337

"When the ruler of the feast had tasted the water that was made wine, and knew not whence it was...the governor of the feast called the bridegroom." — John 2:9 (KJV)

Jesus' first miracle was keeping a party going. Not healing, not deliverance—wine for a wedding. God cares about celebration. He turned washing water into the best wine they'd ever tasted. Sometimes miracles are just about joy. Not every divine intervention is dramatic—some are just about making sure the celebration continues. Your party problem might matter to Jesus more than you think. He saved the best wine for last. Your best might still be coming.

Reflection Question: What celebration needs Jesus to intervene in?

DAY 338

"Lord, now lettest thou thy servant depart in peace, according to thy word: For mine eyes have seen thy salvation." — Luke 2:29-30 (KJV)

Simeon waited his whole life to see the Messiah. Decades of showing up at the temple, hoping today was the day. Then Mary walked in with a baby, and Simeon knew. His waiting ended with worship. Some of you have been waiting so long, you've forgotten what you're waiting for. Simeon shows us that long waits can end suddenly. One ordinary day becomes extraordinary. Your Simeon moment might be closer than you think. The wait makes the worship sweeter.

Reflection Question: What long wait might be about to end in worship?

DAY 339

"And there were in the same country shepherds abiding in the field, keeping watch over their flock by night." — Luke 2:8 (KJV)

Night shift workers got the first Christmas announcement. Not priests, not kings—shepherds. Guys who smelled like sheep heard angels before anyone else. God interrupted their ordinary night with extraordinary news. Your night shift might be your invitation to glory. That ordinary job, that mundane routine—it might be exactly where angels want to visit. The shepherds weren't seeking spiritual experiences; they were just working. Glory interrupted their graveyard shift. Sometimes joy shows up at work, not worship.

Reflection Question: How might your ordinary night become extraordinary?

DAY 340

"When they saw the star, they rejoiced with exceeding great joy." —
Matthew 2:10 (KJV)

"Exceeding great joy"—that's redundant on purpose. They'd traveled maybe two years, following a star, probably looking crazy. Then they saw it stop. Their joy exceeded great; it was exceeding great. Long journeys make arrival sweeter. They could have quit a hundred times, concluded the star was coincidence. But they kept following, and exceeding great joy was their reward. Your long journey toward promise might be near its exceeding great joy moment. Stars are easier to follow in darkness.

Reflection Question: What star have you been following that's about to stop over promise?

DAY 341

"Also in the fifteenth day of the seventh month, when ye have gathered in the fruit of the land, ye shall keep a feast unto the Lord seven days." —
Leviticus 23:39 (KJV)

God commanded parties. Seven-day celebrations. Not suggested—commanded. After harvest, take a week and celebrate. God knows you need structured celebration, not just random rejoicing. When's your last seven-day celebration? Not vacation—celebration. Intentional joy, structured thanksgiving, commanded party time. You feel guilty taking a day off, and God's commanding week-long festivals. Some obedience looks like celebration.

Reflection Question: What harvest in your life deserves a commanded celebration?

DAY 342

"And bring hither the fatted calf, and kill it; and let us eat, and be merry: For this my son was dead, and is alive again." — Luke 15:23-24 (KJV)

The father threw a party for failure. The son who wasted everything got the fatted calf. The older brother was furious—parties should be for performers, not prodigals. But the father celebrates returns, not records. Your failure might qualify you for a party. The very thing that should disqualify you might be what causes heaven's celebration. God throws parties for prodigals, not perfect people. Heaven celebrates your return more than your record.

Reflection Question: What return deserves a party despite the record?

DAY 343

"My heart rejoiceth in the Lord, mine horn is exalted in the Lord: my mouth is enlarged over mine enemies." — 1 Samuel 2:1 (KJV)

Hannah went from barren to blessing, from mockery to mother. Her response wasn't quiet gratitude—it was a song that still echoes. "My mouth is enlarged"—she got louder in celebration than she'd been in sorrow. Your breakthrough deserves volume. Hannah shows us that answered prayers should be louder than asking prayers. She was mocked for years; now her mouth was enlarged over enemies. Let your celebration be proportional to your suffering. Barrenness makes birth announcements louder.

Reflection Question: What breakthrough deserves a louder celebration?

DAY 344

"And Miriam the prophetess, the sister of Aaron, took a timbrel in her hand; and all the women went out after her with timbrels and with dances."
— *Exodus 15:20 (KJV)*

Miriam packed a tambourine for the exodus. Through slavery, plagues, and midnight escapes, she carried an instrument. That's faith—bringing celebration equipment to your deliverance before it happens. What are you packing for your exodus? Miriam expected to need that tambourine. She planned for joy before seeing the sea part. Your celebration might be waiting for you to pack for it. Faith brings tambourines to trials.

Reflection Question: What celebration equipment do you need to pack in faith?

DAY 345

"Weeping may endure for a night, but joy cometh in the morning." —
Psalm 30:5 (KJV)

Joy has an appointment with your morning. Not might come, not hopefully comes—cometh. It's scheduled, confirmed, guaranteed. Your weeping has an expiration time: night. Joy has an arrival time: morning. Some of you have been in a long night. Feels like morning forgot your address. But David says joy cometh. Present tense, active, on its way. Your night might be a season, but morning is programmed into creation. Sunrise is certain. So is your joy.

Reflection Question: What night is about to surrender to morning joy?

DAY 346

"Then he said unto them, Go your way, eat the fat, and drink the sweet, and send portions unto them for whom nothing is prepared...for the joy of the Lord is your strength." — Nehemiah 8:10 (KJV)

They were crying over God's word, convicted and broken. Nehemiah said stop crying, start celebrating. Eat fat, drink sweet, share with others. Sometimes the spiritual thing is to stop weeping and start feasting. "The joy of the Lord is your strength"—not your determination, not your discipline—joy. You're trying to be strong through willpower when God offers strength through joy. That celebration you're postponing might be the strength you're missing. Joy is a strength strategy, not just an emotion.

Reflection Question: Where do you need joy-strength instead of willpower-strength?

DAY 347

"But Paul and Silas were praying and singing hymns to God, and the prisoners were listening to them." — Acts 16:25 (KJV)

Midnight. Maximum security. Backs bleeding. They sang. Not whispered—the other prisoners heard them. Joy in jail confuses everyone, including jailers. Their celebration didn't match their circumstances. Your prison might need a song. Not because you feel musical but because joy in jail is jailbreaking. Their singing caused an earthquake. Your joy in bondage might shake foundations too. Prisoners are listening to how you handle imprisonment.

Reflection Question: What prison needs your singing to shake its foundations?

DAY 348

"And the ransomed of the Lord shall return, and come to Zion with songs and everlasting joy upon their heads." — Isaiah 35:10 (KJV)

The ransomed return with songs, with everlasting joy on their heads like crowns. Not temporary joy, not cautious optimism—everlasting joy. The return journey is a celebration parade. You've been ransomed. Your return to promise should be loud with songs. Joy isn't just an emotion; it's your crown. Wear it. Let everyone see that ransomed people return differently than they left. Everlasting joy looks good on ransomed heads.

Reflection Question: What return needs to be celebrated with everlasting joy?

DAY 349

"And Sarah said, God hath made me to laugh, so that all that hear will laugh with me." — Genesis 21:6 (KJV)

Sarah went from sarcastic laughter to sincere laughter. Same sound, different source. Her mockery became merriment. God turned her doubt into delight. Now everyone who hears her story laughs with her, not at her. Your sarcastic "yeah right" might become sincere celebration. The very thing you laughed at in disbelief might become what you laugh about in joy. Sarah named him Isaac—"laughter"—making her joy permanent. God specializes in turning sarcasm into celebration.

Reflection Question: What sarcastic laughter is God converting to sincere joy?

DAY 350

"Thou preparest a table before me in the presence of mine enemies: my soul shall be satisfied as with marrow and fatness." — Psalm 23:5 (KJV)

God doesn't prepare tables in private. He sets them up where your enemies can see. Your celebration becomes their education. The ones who counted you out have to watch you feast. That public vindication you're waiting for—it's being set like a table. Your enemies don't get invited, but they get to watch. Sometimes joy is the best revenge. Not vengeful joy, but visible joy that proves God provides. Tables in enemy presence taste better.

Reflection Question: What table is God preparing that your enemies will have to witness?

DAY 351

"And suddenly there was with the angel a multitude of the heavenly host praising God, and saying, Glory to God in the highest." — Luke 2:13-14 (KJV)

Heaven couldn't contain its joy. One angel delivered the message, then the whole choir showed up uninvited. They couldn't help themselves. Some news demands spontaneous celebration. When did heaven last crash your party? Maybe you haven't been celebrating enough to attract angels. The shepherds got an angel flash mob because heaven knew they'd receive it. Your celebration might be so small, heaven doesn't notice. Some joy is so big, heaven joins in.

Reflection Question: What celebration in your life deserves heaven's choir?

DAY 352

"And, behold, thou shalt be dumb, and not able to speak, until the day that these things shall be performed, because thou believest not my words." — *Luke 1:20 (KJV)*

Zechariah went mute for doubting joy. Nine months of silence because he couldn't believe good news. When John was born, his first words were praise. Sometimes God silences doubt so joy can grow undisturbed. Your silence might be preparation for celebration. That season where you can't speak, can't explain, can't defend—maybe God's growing something worth singing about. Zechariah's first words after silence were worship. Some joy needs silence to incubate.

Reflection Question: What silence is preparing you for celebration?

DAY 353

"These things have I spoken unto you, that my joy might remain in you, and that your joy might be full." — *John 15:11 (KJV)*

Jesus wants your joy full, not partial. Not half-empty, not mostly full—full. His joy remaining in you fills what your joy can't. It's like having two tanks—yours might be empty, but His is always full. You're operating on partial joy, rationing celebration like it's scarce. But Jesus offers full joy—topped off, overflowing, complete. The things He spoke were specifically designed to fill your joy tank. Full joy is available. Stop settling for partial.

Reflection Question: What area needs filling with His joy, not just yours?

DAY 354

"For the kingdom of God is not meat and drink; but righteousness, and peace, and joy in the Holy Ghost." — Romans 14:17 (KJV)

The Kingdom ingredients: righteousness, peace, and joy. Not rules, regulations, and religion. Joy is literally part of the Kingdom recipe. Without joy, you're not fully experiencing the Kingdom. Some of you have righteousness and peace but no joy. That's two-thirds Kingdom. Joy isn't optional; it's constitutional. The Holy Ghost brings joy as standard equipment, not optional upgrade. The Kingdom is joyful, or it's not the Kingdom.

Reflection Question: Which Kingdom ingredient—righteousness, peace, or joy—are you missing?

DAY 355

"Rejoice in the Lord alway: and again I say, Rejoice." — Philippians 4:4 (KJV)

Paul said it twice because once wasn't enough. Rejoice always. Then, in case you missed it: Rejoice. From prison. The guy in chains is telling free people to celebrate. That's apostolic audacity. "Always" doesn't mean "when you feel like it." It means now, in this, despite that. Rejoicing is a discipline, not just a feeling. Paul proved you can rejoice in chains, so you can rejoice in your situation. If Paul said it twice, it's twice as important.

Reflection Question: What "always" situation needs rejoicing despite appearances?

DAY 356

"Your father Abraham rejoiced to see my day: and he saw it, and was glad."
— John 8:56 (KJV)

Abraham saw Jesus' day thousands of years early and rejoiced. He celebrated promise before fulfillment, saw the invisible and threw a party. That's faith—celebrating what you can't see yet. What future day can you see by faith? Abraham's ability to see forward caused present joy. Your promise might be distant, but you can rejoice now for what's coming then. Future joy can be accessed in present faith.

Reflection Question: What future promise deserves present rejoicing?

DAY 357

"He that goeth forth and weepeth, bearing precious seed, shall doubtless come again with rejoicing, bringing his sheaves with him." — *Psalm 126:6*
(KJV)

You sowed in tears. Every seed was watered with weeping. The planting season was brutal. But the psalmist says "doubtless"—no question, guaranteed, certainly—you'll return rejoicing. Your tear-watered seeds are growing. The harvest from your hardest season will be your happiest celebration. "Bringing his sheaves"—not returning empty but loaded with harvest. Your weeping was investment, not waste. Tears are just pre-joy irrigation.

Reflection Question: What tears are about to become rejoicing harvest?

DAY 358

"O sing unto the Lord a new song; for he hath done marvellous things." —
Psalm 98:1 (KJV)

New song for new things. Your old playlist doesn't fit your new season. God's done marvelous things that deserve fresh music. Stop singing old sadness when God's writing new gladness. You're stuck on repeat with old songs of failure, pain, disappointment. But marvelous things have happened since then. Your testimony needs an update. Your worship needs new lyrics. Marvelous things deserve new songs.

Reflection Question: What marvelous thing deserves a new song?

DAY 359

"For unto you is born this day in the city of David a Saviour, which is
Christ the Lord." — Luke 2:11 (KJV)

"Unto you"—personal delivery. Not unto them, unto everyone else—unto you. The Savior's birth announcement has your name on it. Christmas isn't generic; it's personal. He came for you specifically. Tonight (whenever you're reading this), remember it's unto you. The shepherds weren't special, weren't expecting it, weren't ready. But the angel said "unto you." Your Savior was born for you, specifically, personally. Christmas is God saying "unto you" to everyone.

Reflection Question: How does "unto you" change how you see Christmas?

DAY 360

"Glory to God in the highest, and on earth peace, good will toward men."
— Luke 2:14 (KJV)

Heaven's birth announcement was three-fold: glory up, peace down, good will around. That's the Christmas formula. When God gets glory, earth gets peace, and people get good will. You're trying to manufacture peace without giving glory. Attempting good will without worship. The angels showed us the sequence: glory first, then peace and good will follow. Your chaos might be a glory deficit. Christmas mathematics: Glory + Peace + Good Will = Joy.

Reflection Question: Where do you need to give glory to receive peace?

DAY 361

"Hitherto hath the Lord helped us." — 1 Samuel 7:12 (KJV)

"Hitherto"—up to this point. Samuel set up a stone called Ebenezer, meaning "hitherto." Every year needs an Ebenezer— a marker saying, "God helped us make it this far." Look back. Where did God help this year? That situation in March that should have ended you. That crisis in July that didn't crash you. Set up your stone. Hitherto—you made it this far. Every December 31st is an Ebenezer opportunity.

Reflection Question: What Ebenezer stone does this year deserve?

DAY 362

"Looking unto Jesus the author and finisher of our faith; who for the joy that was set before him endured the cross." — Hebrews 12:2 (KJV)

Jesus endured the cross because of future joy. He saw past Friday to Sunday, past cross to crown. Future joy gave Him present endurance. He celebrated victory before fighting the battle. Your cross might be bearable if you could see your coming joy. Jesus proves that future joy has present power. What you're enduring has an expiration date. Joy is scheduled after this cross. Future joy funds present endurance.

Reflection Question: What future joy helps you endure the present cross?

DAY 363

"And when they had opened their treasures, they presented unto him gifts; gold, and frankincense, and myrrh." — Matthew 2:11 (KJV)

They brought funeral spice to a baby shower. Myrrh was for burial. Strange gift, unless you know the whole story. They celebrated His birth while acknowledging His purpose. Sometimes joy and sorrow share the same space. Your celebration might be bittersweet. Joy mixed with awareness of future pain. That's okay. The wise men teach us that you can celebrate and stay realistic. Bring your gold and your myrrh. Honest joy acknowledges the whole story.

Reflection Question: What bittersweet gift do you need to offer?

DAY 364

"Fear not: for, behold, I bring you good tidings of great joy, which shall be to all people." — Luke 2:10 (KJV)

Not just joy—GREAT joy. The angel could have said joy, but added the adjective. Christmas joy isn't ordinary; it's great. And it's for all people—including you. Especially you. Your joy doesn't have to be moderate. The angel announced great joy, so receive great joy. Not cautious happiness, not careful celebration—great joy. Heaven doesn't do small when announcing salvation. Great joy is your inheritance. Claim it.

Reflection Question: Where are you settling for small joy when great joy is available?

DAY 365

"This is the day which the Lord hath made; we will rejoice and be glad in it." — Psalm 118:24 (KJV)

Every day is God-made, including the last one of the year. "We WILL rejoice"—not might, not should—will. It's a decision, not a feeling. The psalmist chose gladness before knowing how the day would go. Tomorrow starts a new year, but today still belongs to God. Don't wait for January 1 to rejoice. This day, even if it's the year's last, deserves gladness. God made it; that's reason enough. End with joy. Begin with joy. Fill the middle with joy.

Reflection Question: How will you rejoice in this God-made day?

OUR BOOKS

Start each day with purpose, peace, and spiritual renewal.

Whether you're walking solo, side by side with a partner, or seeking strength for the journey ahead—this devotional series meets you right where you are.

Collect the Whole Series

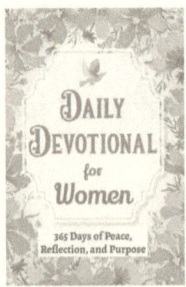 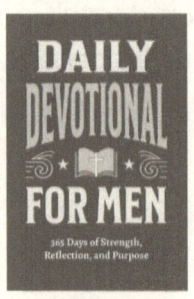 

Daily Devotional for Women

Daily Devotional for Men

Daily Devotional for Couples

Available at:

- Amazon

- Barnes & Noble

- Major online bookstores

Each book is a spiritual companion. Together, they form a complete journey—personal, relational, and transformative.

Don't wait—bring home the full devotional set and let every day draw you closer to faith, love, and lasting renewal.